Literature-based
reading programs at work

Literature-based
reading programs at work

edited by
Joelie Hancock and Susan Hill

with a foreword by
Priscilla Lynch

Heinemann
Portsmouth, NH

Heinemann Educational Books, Inc.
70 Court Street, Portsmouth, NH 03801
Offices and agents throughout the world

Library of Congress Cataloging-in-Publication Data

Literature-based reading programs at work / edited by Joelie Hancock
    and Susan Hill.
        p. cm.
    ISBN 0-435-08466-6
    1. Children—Books and reading. 2. Children's literature—Study
and teaching. 3. School libraries—Activity programs. I. Hancock,
Joelie. II. Hill, Susan.
Z1037.A1L57 1987
372.6′4—dc19   87-33627
                                                        CIP

Printed in the United States of America
10 9 8 7 6 5 4 3 2 1

Contents

Acknowledgements

Acknowledgements for permission to reproduce published material are due as follows: *Teacher* for the Reading Conference Record in Chapter 5; Ashton Scholastic for Holdaway's 'Steps in a Conference', Chapter 5; Methuen Australia for the cover of Watt and Roberts, *The Animals that Loved Reading*, shown in Chapter 4. We also acknowledge the support of the South Australian College of Advanced Education and Ray Stradwick who took most of the photographs within the text.

Foreword

This is a book about change, specifically about teachers, administrators, specialists, and parents making the change from a basal-based reading program to a literature-based reading program. It is a book about beliefs, about teachers' questions and answers, and about problems and solutions.

The change agents in this book are new teachers and experienced teachers, primary and secondary teachers, coordinators and administrators, plus teacher/librarians. (Teacher/librarians are those educators who have had special training in library science, usually a fifth year, and divide their time between the classroom and the library.)

What is particularly valuable in the articles in this book are the detailed explanations of how these educators made the change:
- [ ] step-by-step suggestions for initiating a literature-based reading program,
- [ ] recommendations for selecting and obtaining materials,
- [ ] alternatives for the physical arrangement of classrooms,
- [ ] organizational patterns that work,
- [ ] ideas for making the transition a smooth one for children,
- [ ] ways of enlisting the aid of school resource people and parents in the transition,
- [ ] and, above all, explanations of *why* the transition should be made.

Change can be uncomfortable, perhaps even threatening, to many of us. All too often, in the school setting, we are *told* to change, not *asked* to change. All too often we are excluded from decisions. We are told that new materials have been purchased and that we must use them, without ever having examined them ahead of time. Change is imposed on us, and we feel powerless. When we feel powerless, we feel threatened, and that makes us tend to resist change.

For any change to be effective, we have to feel it's a good idea. That means we have to be consulted ahead of time about the changes. We have to have time to see the new ideas in action, to listen to those who have already made the transition, to read about the research underlying the change, to talk with our colleagues, and to think through what is being suggested and how we can do it. We have to have our questions answered and our concerns addressed, whether they are voiced or not.

We worry about what will be altered in our beliefs. What will be required of us? How will we be prepared for this change? How will we be evaluated? What already existing materials and strategies do we have that will fit into the suggested changes? What do we already know and know how to do that we can build on? The articles in this book demonstrate, reassuringly, how these questions have been asked and answered in a variety of school contexts.

After all, change is not an event; it is a *process*. Change does not lie in educational materials. It comes about when individuals alter their beliefs and adapt their actions to accommodate those beliefs. The contributors to this book examined their beliefs, asked questions, looked for answers, and expressed their concerns before creating change. Some of them arrived at a literature-based reading program through a personal study of new research. Some made the transition because they realized their children "weren't really enjoying their reading."

Some made changes in just one classroom, and others were involved in changes in a whole school. Each article details a different situation.

What is the same in all the articles, however, is the educators' conviction that books are their own reward and that children reap that reward by having time every day to read whole books and respond to them in their own personal way. This reflects a fundamental change in the educators' beliefs, a paradigm shift from a behavioristic to a developmental approach to reading. Because literature-based reading programs have been in effect for some time in Australia and New Zealand, we have a tendency to forget that teachers in these countries started out progressing sequentially through basal readers, just as we have done. They had to go through exactly the same anxiety, tentativeness, and experimentation all teachers go through on the way to making the conversion to a literature-based reading program. This book reflects that journey in detail.

They, too, were trained in the behavioristic approach, which made them regard real books as ancillary to the required sequential basal readers. For them, too, the basal readers, the workbooks, the reproducible materials, and the tests *were* the reading program. They, too, believed that they had to start out presenting isolated, fragmented bits of language to children. They used the behavioristic stimulus/response process, which is directly antithetical to the way a child learns to talk, or to do anything else, for that matter.

For these educators, and for many of us, the desire to change to a literature-based reading program has been prompted by the realization that although our children can read, they don't, not voluntarily. Reading a book is not a first-choice activity for our children; in fact, reading a book is not even among the first five first-choice activities selected by our children. They would rather do five other things than read a book.

Reading, in their eyes, is something done in a group for a very short time each day, using a basal reader written in "readabilitized language." The length of the words, the number of syllables, the length of the sentences, and the total vocabulary are controlled. Pronouns are substituted for nouns; causal connectors are removed, making it difficult for children to recognize links between sentences; and the illustrations carry the meaning. This kind of language is hard for children because they cannot use anything of what they already know about language, which is considerable. They cannot apply their prior knowledge, and so they often experience failure.

Because the basal stories are written to incorporate a specific skill, not to engage a child's heart and mind, they are not very interesting. These short stories do not allow children to experience the purpose and pleasure of real reading. Books, interesting books, are often available to our children only as rewards, *after* they have finished their work. And as a result, fluent readers practice reading and become more fluent, while less fluent readers are deprived of the practice they so need. They are given more lessons, more workbook pages, and more tests. They experience more loss of self-esteem and come to look upon reading as something to be avoided.

Fortunately there is a wealth of new research available that will help us in our search for a more productive way of teaching reading and giving children a reason for learning to read. And fortunately, there is a book like this one with concrete suggestions for making that search easier. **Shayne O'Halloran** gives us a reading survey she uses at the beginning of the year to find out her students' likes, dislikes, and attitudes toward reading. The survey gives her the information she needs to match up students and books. **Helen Kerin** gives us a model letter to parents, with clear suggestions about helping at home. **Kathleen Graham** details the steps taken during an individual reading conference to make that time become a sharing, learning time for both teacher and student. **Meredith Kennedy** gives us her Personal Questionnaire/Reading Inventory that she uses to get to know her students.

The settings in this book range from a "reception class" of very young children, right through the elementary grades. **Pat Smith** wanted to duplicate as closely as possible the conditions in which her "Preps" had learned to talk, and she tells us about setting up the physical environment needed to produce those conditions for very young children. **Andrew Phillips** writes about his need to persuade his group of older students that reading was not just basal readers, short stories, and reading in a group. He started out by piling a collection of very good books on a table so that his students would have to handle and sample a lot of books before selecting one.

Although many of the book titles suggested in the articles are Australian, the suggestions for using them are useful for any books in any classroom. **Deirdre Travers** uses Australian titles in studying themes with her students, but the themes themselves are universal ("country and city life," "man and his environment," "against the odds," and "myself and others") and can be used with different titles that reflect the culture and experiences of other students. **Sue Le Busque** writes about using poetry and biography with her students. One or two of the biographies concern Australian personalities, but the ideas and strategies outlined in the article can be used with any poetry and any biographies. **Trish Ditz**, on the other hand, writes about using fairy tales and folklore with her students, and those are books that belong to all children and are available to all of us. The important thing is not the titles, but the strategies used to introduce children to the wealth of children's books they can read.

Teachers who are accustomed to using basal readers are almost always uncertain about how they will evaluate students' performances if they move into a literature-based reading program. Tests, evaluations, and precise measurements have always played a major role in the behaviorists' approach to reading. When language is broken down into small bits, it's easy to measure. The question is, of course, what are we measuring?

If we're measuring children's recognition of the long sound of *a*, the tests are adequate. If, however, we're measuring children's comprehension, their ability to use their prior knowledge to make meaning, and their ability to use repair strategies when meaning breaks down, then the tests are not adequate. The authors in this book use pre- and postsurveys of attitude and preferences, student journals, their own conference notes, students' writing samples, students' original projects, tapes and their own observations, all of which have more validity and reliability than standardized tests. Their measuring instruments measure children's reading, not simply their grasp of the surface structure of language, and the instruments are easy to use, given the time constraints of the average day.

Teachers making the shift to literature-based reading programs are also concerned with how they will make sure all their children will "get the skills," and "get the vocabulary." **Meredith Kennedy** sets out a particularly helpful description of integrating skills, vocabulary, reading, and writing into her literature program. Teachers worry about time, always. Several of the articles in this book address this worry directly, outlining schedules that may be used to insure adequate time for every area of reading instruction and learning. And several of the articles are organized around a question-and-answer format, so we see our own concerns voiced right there in black and white. Each of these educators has gone through the transition process. Each speaks to us in a distinct, individual voice, and we recognize the words.

This book is reassuring. Here are a variety of educators—new and experienced teachers, teacher/librarians working in public and private schools, reading consultants—all with varied resources available to them. As we read, we can find parallels to our own experiences, our school plants, our administrative organizations, and our different levels of understanding and acceptance of the developmental learn-to-read-by-reading approach. Each article contains something we can use right now.

Change requires that we start where we are at the moment in our own knowledge. It requires that we take one step at a time, in our own individual style and at our own rate of learning, doing as much as we can to experience success. The process of change is not easy, but reading about others who have changed makes the transition a good deal easier and smoother for us.

Priscilla Lynch

Introduction

This book is about teachers planning, carrying out and evaluating reading programs that are based on using 'real' books rather than basal reading schemes. Teachers and teacher-librarians write about how they have used literature in their classes to develop their students' reading.

All these teachers have similar reasons for using a wide range of literature in their reading programs. Primarily they believe that reading can and should be its own reward. The key to a successful reading program is in providing a wide range of enriching, satisfying books and helping children to find their own rewards in these books.

Providing a range of worthwhile reading materials is essential; time to read and talk about them is just as important. Through talking about books, students find out other readers' reactions to the same books and to other books. They also become a community of readers where books and understandings from books are shared. They learn what it is to be a lifelong reader: the pleasures, the choices, the strategies and the sharing. And they learn to read by reading.

The developmental learn-to-read-by-reading approach used in these classrooms is based on Don Holdaway's *Independence in Reading* (Ashton Scholastic, 1979) — still the most useful resource in understanding this orientation to teaching reading. Holdaway's recommendations are based on observations of supportive home environments in which young children learnt to read. The supportive literacy environment, he writes, includes a large supply of reading materials, regular opportunities to hear books read aloud and an adult who enjoys reading and responds to the readers' questions about books and print.

Good books and time to read and talk about them are common to all the programs described here. But there is more to teaching reading than that. Each teacher makes decisions about how to find out about the children's reading, how to organise the classroom, what input to give the children, what the class will do apart from reading and talking about the books, and how to monitor each child's reading. The articles in this book are about the decisions that some teachers have made for their classes.

The first set of articles is about teachers setting up literature-based programs. **Shayne O'Halloran** has been using this approach to reading for many years, and now has a clear framework for planning with a new class. She also knows what concerns teachers about the approach — and from her experience provides answers for their questions. **Helen Kerin** tells how over a year her focus changed from setting up a favorable environment, selecting books, finding out about the children, and informing parents to organising for independent and integrated reading. **Pat Smith** writes how after several years away from the classroom, she began a reception class with a literature-based program.

The next two articles are by teachers who do not have their own class but have helped to introduce literature-based reading into their schools. **Shirley Yeates**, as the Language Arts co-ordinator in her school, introduced the approach to the whole school and supported several teachers in their initial stages. **Kathleen Graham** is teacher-librarian and came from a school where literature-based reading was already established. She introduced the approach to her new school, already aware of the steps she would take in gaining the staff's confidence, in having them accept her in their classrooms and in supporting their early organisation, conferencing and book selection.

The teachers in the second section of the book write about particular focuses they have taken in their programs. **Trish Ditz** chose to focus for several weeks on fairy tales with a year 7 class and **Sue Le Busque** chose poetry and biography for year 6/7s. **Andrew Phillips** introduced Australian short stories, historical fiction, science fiction and biographies to a year 7 class to broaden their reading interests before high school. To encourage deeper responses and discussion from their readers, **Deirdre Travers** focused her program with year 7s on themes such as 'Man and his Environment' and 'Against the Odds', while **Beverley Endersbee** based her program on Roald Dahl's books. **Meredith Kennedy** describes how she linked writing activities with a reading program and **Maria Woodhouse** writes about a Big Book and poetry emphasis with her year 3 class.

Teachers implement literature-based reading programs in ways that suit their own strengths, their interests and their perceptions of what could benefit their particular students. The accounts of these teachers show that their reading programs, using a range of selected literature, not only enhance their students' reading abilities but also help to develop keen and appreciative lifelong readers. We hope that this book will help more teachers and children share the excitement and pleasure of good literature.

Susan Hill and Joelie Hancock

Beginning a literature-based program

An experienced teacher tells how   1

Shayne O'Halloran

I grew to love reading from an early age. I escaped the various problems of living in a provincial town through burying myself in books. Reading still remains my chief hobby, and it was with my own childhood in mind that I set up an individualised reading program for my upper primary students. I believe that a love of reading comes from the pleasure experienced when children find books that suit their interests and preferences, and have time to read them in a supportive, relaxed atmosphere. I also believe, with Frank Smith, that children learn to read by reading.

Organisation

I have now worked for six years — five in Australian schools and one in a year 6 class in Canada — at creating a reading program where children can experience the pleasures of reading. Individualising the program and establishing a supportive atmosphere have been essential ingredients. The steps that I take in setting up such a program are these:

- ☐ set up the class library
- ☐ encourage independent selection
- ☐ arrange the learning environment
- ☐ provide time to read
- ☐ share reading experiences
- ☐ stimulate further reading
- ☐ monitor reading development

In the following pages I describe how I go about each of these. I then discuss problems raised by my program and some solutions that have worked for me.

Set up the class library

The first organisational step is to ensure the availability of books. Children must have a choice of books and be exposed to a wide variety during the course of the program.

I recommend a hundred books for a class of thirty, and have found the Ashton Scholastic Core Libraries (1984) an invaluable starting point. They now contain approximately 140 books in three modules for each level, selected in order to provide a balanced variety of literary genres. The interests of particular age groups are considered, as well as the readability levels of the books and the range of reading abilities at any one year level. There will always be some students, however, whose tastes are not met in the class kits, so each month I supplement the Ashton kits with a selection borrowed from the school and town libraries. Usually a group of children makes the selections, a different group each time. The selections always include some of my favorites too!

One year I had access to a school bus and the whole class visited and borrowed from the town library every fortnight. That was very exciting and stimulating for us all. Many of the eleven-year-olds in that class had never visited their local library before, and others had borrowed only rarely. The benefits were immeasurable, not the least being the sharing of a diversity of reading experiences within the class and a resulting interest in new genres. In addition, the path had been laid for the students to regularly borrow from a familiar community library some time in the future.

It is not always possible for teachers to transport their classes to a local library regularly, but it is often possible to take a group of four children in one's own car. I have sometimes done this and found it well worth while. I once divided the class into four interest groups and each fortnight a representative from each group visited the library and borrowed books for the others in his or her group. This fostered great anticipation and planning, leading to the highlight, when thirty carefully selected books arrived. If a chosen book did not appeal to its designated reader, there was often someone else who wanted to read it. However, I have found the children are usually very knowledgeable about their friends' reading habits, and selections are usually relevant to interests.

Books can also enter the classroom in a variety of other ways:

- ☐ Book Club orders
- ☐ donations from parents
- ☐ comic and book swaps
- ☐ loans from homes
- ☐ books written by class members (at times these books, written in the individualised writing program, are preferred to the commercially published variety)

Encourage independent selection

Once the books are available in the classroom, the children must have time to select the ones they would like to read. I am very tolerant of the children's choices and allow comics, magazines, picture books and adult fiction. However, a goal of my program is for all the children to become responsible selectors and to increase the number and variety of books they read. I do this by providing plenty of books, and whenever possible, casually directing them to more challenging material and quality literature.

For me, 'quality' literature entertains, informs and uses language in ways that captivate the reader. I develop selection skills by promoting a wide range of literature in the classroom, with posters, book displays and with radio and television programs that promote books. But most valuable of all is word of mouth. Talking about books becomes a natural part of the children's conversations in and outside the classroom.

Arrange the learning environment

The learning environment is important if an individualised reading program is to work well. Schools in which it is easy to run an individualised program are those that encourage conversation, foster individual interests and creativity, minimise evaluation requirements and competition, and possess well stocked, accessible libraries and bookrooms, with accommodating librarians.

Schools which rigidly adhere to a set and formalised basal reading program may not allow the freedom necessary for a totally individualised program. But the teacher can in most instances supplement formalised reading at some stage during the school week with reading selected by the children themselves. Time can always be found for activities that a teacher really believes to be important.

I had not realised the importance of the physical environment for reading until I read my students' responses to a survey I gave at the beginning of my year in Canada. (See below for the questions asked.) The answers to questions 15 to 18 showed that nearly all of my students preferred to read at home because they could be in bed or on a couch, and also eat while they were reading. Five students said the school seats were too hard and they did not like to sit at desks to read. Making an area inviting for reading is not always easy. The architecture and layout of my room in Canada, although in a new school, were designed for rows of desks; there weren't any 'soft' spots in the whole room. Children were allocated desks and there they stayed; there was no room for anything else. In contrast, my Australian classroom had more comfortable chairs, and tables organised into groups, and allowed for a secluded reading corner stuffed with plenty of old cushions, pillows and bean bags. The children always looked relaxed in this 'homey' corner.

READING SURVEY

(used with year 6 class)

NAME ....

True or False

		T	F
1	Most books are too long and dull	☐	☐
2	There should be more free reading in school	☐	☐
3	Reading is as important as television	☐	☐
4	Reading is boring	☐	☐
5	Reading is rewarding to me	☐	☐
6	I think reading is fun	☐	☐
7	Teachers ask me to read books that are too hard	☐	☐
8	I am a poor reader	☐	☐
9	My parents spend quite a bit of time reading	☐	☐
10	My brothers and/or sisters read often	☐	☐

Finish these sentences
11 I would read one book every ....
12 My favorite book is ....
13 I like to read books about ....
14 Some of my favorite authors are ....
   ....
15 I **like** or **dislike** to read because ....
   ....
16 When I read I ....
17 I **like** or **dislike** to read at home because ....
   ....
18 I **like** or **dislike** to read at school because ....
   ....
19 The things that attract me to a book are ....
   ....

Answer these questions
20 How often do you read at home? ....
21 How often do you watch TV at home? ....
22 When was the last time you received a book as a gift? ....

Provide time to read

Time must be provided for the children to read at school. This is necessary because many children do not read at home and therefore have no regular time to read. If readers are going to develop their reading skills and a love of reading, then they do need to have uninterrupted time to read.

The reading survey also showed how infrequently many of the children read at home. Eight children read approximately one book a week, six read a book every two or three weeks, and sixteen — more than half the class — rarely read a book in a month. Several of these children did not voluntarily read any books in a year, while *everyone* watched television daily.

Schools must counter the influence of television and video as the major recreational pursuits in the home, by providing time for reading. Twenty to thirty minutes a day of Uninterrupted Silent Sustained Reading (USSR) works with my upper primary pupils, although I usually start the program with shorter daily periods. These periods are lengthened when students appear to be able to cope with this new-found freedom.

Share reading experiences

Children like to talk to each other about their reading experiences and favorite books. This occurs informally after silent reading and whenever free activity and natural talk arise. It should be mentioned that I value the learning potential of talk, and therefore allow my class greater latitude for talk and movement than most teachers do.

Sharing also occurs formally during class talking and listening sessions. Children are regularly encouraged to tell the whole class about their reading. This is often done through simply telling what the book is about. It is surprising the interest and talk generated from retelling. Other children in the class who have read the book volunteer information, their likes and their dislikes. The discussion between these children and others whose interest has been awakened can be very productive.

Follow-up activities based on a finished book have never been given a high priority in my program, as I've found that often children do not want to do an expected response-after-a-book activity. Many activities designed for this purpose appear to be a form of assessment, as though the reading has not been sufficiently successful if a child immediately wants to read another. I am perfectly satisfied that the reader has gained something of value if he or she wants to find another book when the first choice has been finished.

Stimulate further reading

I have never found difficulty in stimulating recreational reading. The most significant ways I do this are:

☐ I read aloud every day, often allowing the class to choose the book. Usually I serialise complete novels but occasionally I will read selected excerpts and short stories.

☐ My class sees me read during USSR. I read children's literature, professional reading or adult novels. I hope I model what I would like them to do — read widely. The children are thus aware that I too value reading, and this helps them appreciate its importance.

☐ I am not judgemental of what children read, and allow all tastes into my room. The children see their choices and opinions valued and respected and are therefore not threatened by the program. An additional advantage is that the greater the variety of interest displayed in the room, the greater the stimulus on each child to widen his or her reading. Peer influence is a great stimulus in any learning situation and individualised reading is no exception.

Monitor reading development

I believe that testing and comprehension exercises should be minimised in individualised reading programs. It is important that recreational reading not be labelled as 'work', and this can be avoided if care is taken in the way reading is assessed. I fully agree with a recent comment by Canadian Bill Martin at a conference in 1985, that 'good literature should not be done to death . . . it should be able to stand on its own'. He warns teachers not to kill children's interest in reading by scrutinising it obtrusively for assessment.

However, sometimes there are assessment demands that must be met and it is certainly important for teachers to know how each child is progressing in an individualised program. How then can teachers best assess such a program?

There is a reliable, valid and painless way, and that is through observation of the readers' attitudes, interests and borrowing patterns, and regularly recording these observations. The children's own reading records can be helpful. I train the children to keep lists of the books they have read and these lists enable me to keep track of developments in interests. They each have a *Books I have read* sheet ruled into four columns:

Title   *Author*   *Location*   *Comment*

'Location' refers to where the book came from. The children are encouraged to fill the list in at least once a week, and when the page is full they staple a new one over it. I realise this assumes a degree of responsibility that some children may not yet possess, so I usually have these sheets pasted onto a card on the wall where they stay for the year. Both the children and I then have easy access to what the children are reading, and they are being taught a valuable skill of record-keeping.

Individual reading conferences are important in monitoring reading progress, strategies and interests. They allow for comprehension to be assessed through retelling, answering questions and discussion. In addition, they have a positive effect on the students, who receive encouragement, share their reactions to books and realise that the teacher is genuinely interested in their reading.

In each day's reading session I usually plan a half hour of activity when the children work independently and I can conference individual children without interruption. The activities might include process writing, an activity with words or formal work from a stencil or the board. In half an hour I can conference six children and so can talk to all of them about their reading each week.

When I began conferencing, I found the Ashton library kits an invaluable aid. Each book from the kit has a page in a ringed folder which summarises the plot and provides comprehension/discussion questions for the teacher to select from. These are great time-savers for the busy teacher, and valuable aids in assessing a reader's understanding. However, it is not difficult to gauge a reader's comprehension of a book I haven't read. If the child can retell the plot and describe the characters to me, I am generally satisfied. Because I don't know the book, I have a genuine interest in what it's about.

Rigorous application of Bloom's taxonomy of cognitive skills in asking comprehension questions can be self-defeating, as can any other structured or lengthy form of assessment. If poorly handled, assessment can kill interest that has been generated by a book. Children often feel threatened by evaluation, especially when they do not see themselves as successful. It has always been my aim to provide a secure, unthreatening conference time, where talking about books is experienced as a pleasure. The tone is one of sharing rather than testing.

Questions teachers ask

It is not easy to set up an individualised program. In fact it creates more work for the teacher than following a basal reading scheme. In addition, the teacher needs to have a firm understanding of why this sort of program is preferable and what difference it will make, since colleagues and parents will have many doubts and questions. The questions and objections put to me by my colleagues, particularly those in Canada, have been about the following:

☐ children's choices
☐ reluctant readers
☐ interruptions in USSR
☐ reading conferences
☐ time to record
☐ time to conference
☐ lack of direction
☐ reading improvement

I hope my answers to the questions will help teachers who are willing to take on this type of reading program, to be fore-armed.

Don't some children make terrible choices?

My experiences have reinforced my conviction that the teacher should not stop a child from reading a chosen book. The teacher's job is to provide the range and gradually extend the students' interests, without restricting the students' choices. The following episode reinforced my view that children gravitate to their own level and will do this as long as there are suitable books available.

An eleven-year-old in my class was reading one of her mother's books in Silent Reading. It was obviously adult fiction and not the sort of book I would have recommended to her. Another teacher who saw her reading it later said in shocked tones: 'You're not allowing her to read that! I wouldn't allow my sixteen-year-old to read that book when she wanted to. It has very explicit sex scenes'. I felt threatened by the teacher's attitude to my *laissez-faire* approach but I let the girl continue with the book. She was a very mature eleven-year-old, and an attention-seeker. She persevered with the blockbuster for two days before laying it aside for one of James Herriot's books — also taken from her mother's shelves.

I also saw a small group of children whose choices for lengthy periods were magazines, such as *Hit Parader* and *Rock Fever*, and comics. During the course of the year, however, I was able to redirect them to books that were equally appealing to them, and more worthwhile.

Surely some kids will never like reading?

Breakthroughs in turning reluctant readers into enthusiastic book promoters come in many forms. One boy in my class had shown little interest in reading books. All he ever brought to school was comics and magazines. Of course when children know they have to read they will make it bearable for themselves. One day his mother dragged him along to a library promotion and he met Gordon Korman, a children's author. Forunately our Ashton Class Library contained a book by this author and the school library held other titles. My student was so fascinated by meeting a real author that he has since read most of Gordon Korman's books. Moreover, the author was soon popular with other children in the class as well.

If the reading program had not been flexible enough to allow a preference for reading this author, I doubt that this child's interest in reading would have developed in this way.

Generally every teacher has some children in her class who actively dislike reading. I had three different groups of such children in the year 6 Canadian class. One group's recent experiences in reading had been unpleasant; in past years they had had to present a monthly book review with the stipulation that a different author be read each month. The second group was made up of capable students who were more interested in other activities, particularly sport. Then there were the academically weak students who did not come to reading readily; they found it difficult and generally saw themselves as 'poor readers'.

My strategies with these students were:
- [ ] no reading conferences at lunch-time or after school
- [ ] no book reviews required
- [ ] point the students to books they are likely to enjoy

For this I needed to find out the interests and reading preferences of the reluctant and weaker readers. It is better that they read anything than nothing at all. Humor, realistic fiction and sport almanacs were a good start. It is worth watching for the occasional books that do hold the interest of the less interested readers and use these to find others, which may make them revise their view of what reading offers.

Aren't silent reading sessions often interrupted?

When silent reading is organised on a school-wide basis interruptions are not a problem. When your class is the only one doing USSR and the students don't know what it is about, care must be taken in establishing your basic rules and expectations. The same principles apply for all successful USSR sessions, and where USSR flounders it is because these principles have not been met. The McCrackens (1978) found these common problems when they investigated failing USSR sessions:
- [ ] the teacher does not read during USSR;
- [ ] the troublesome students do not read;
- [ ] there is some other person in the class, such as an aide or a visitor, who doesn't read;
- [ ] there are not enough books and reading materials available;
- [ ] the teacher had given up too soon after initial frustrations.

One year I found that my problem was due to disruptions by a troublesome student. He would make loud noises. I immediately stopped 'Free Reading' and began a grammar lesson — one of the least attractive components of the curriculum. This happened several times before the peer pressure of the majority stopped the problem.

What do you do in a reading conference?

Apart from showing an interest in the students' reading, the conference gives the teacher an opportunity to develop students' critical and interpretative thinking and to help the children relate their reading to their personal experiences. There are many resource books, the Ashton Teacher Resource folder for example, that suggest useful general questions. The questions that I like best to use are those that develop from a genuine interest on my part, but the following are useful to get a reader thinking:
- [ ] What is the author wanting to share with you?
- [ ] What are the people in the story like?
- [ ] Which character do you like? Why?
- [ ] Is there any character you dislike? Why that one?
- [ ] Did the character change through the story?
- [ ] Did you like the ending? Why?
- [ ] What was the most exciting/funny/sad part of the story?
- [ ] Did any part of the story surprise you? Why?

I find it useful to have a list of questions like these displayed in the classroom so that the children can come to their conference prepared. Questions from the Scholastic Library help the teacher beginning to conference. But the more I do it, the better I get at framing questions that engage the children and lead them further into the book. Asking what the book was about is generally a good opener to any conference, and can easily lead to higher levels of discussion.

What does the rest of the class do when you hold conference with one child?

A common criticism of individualised programs is that they appear to be disorganised. In fact they must be very well organised, with the children trained to work independently when the teacher is conferencing. I make sure that the children have activities that can occupy them for half an hour, ensure that they know what to do when the activity is finished, and make it very clear that they are not to interrupt.

When do you find time to record your observations?

I record students' reading behaviour, interests and attitudes immediately after USSR or during conferences. The notes are made in an exercise book with a couple of pages for each child. I date each note, for example:

> 12/8 *Kevin is enjoying a book on model aeroplanes he got from the resource teacher.*
> 6/7 *Jenn is reading yet another fish book.*
> 3/8 *Kyle finished* The Secret of Nimh *yesterday. Now Justin has borrowed it.*
> 21/9 *Trevor hasn't read a book for some weeks. Seems to be exclusively interested in comics these days.*
> 14/10 *Michelle had another book from home ready when she finished* Rumblefish *in USSR. How well organised.*

Teachers not used to recording anecdotal comments about children can find it a chore at first, not convinced of their value, but after several weeks the comments prove to be invaluable records of progress that would otherwise go unnoticed. The sense of achievement that I gained in reading back over my records was matched by the children's pleasure in talking about the books they enjoyed.

Don't individual reading programs lack direction?

Individualised programs are not as chaotic as would appear from first meeting them. The children are reading different books, and the teacher cannot plan what they will be reading from one week to the next, but the progress made feels much more substantial than having a class reading a set number and progression of books. A suggestion or a comment from teacher or class member can send a child off in a new reading direction or spark off a new enthusiasm. Because the children are choosing their reading, there appears to be more engagement with the books read, more willingness to talk about them and a greater confidence in their own reading.

Does an individualised reading program improve reading?

When I have had the program going for a year I have been able to objectively demonstrate an improvement in reading ages of at least a year with all but a few children. The tests that I have used in the past are the Gapadol Reading Comprehension Tests. The results for 1986 are shown in the following table.

PROGRESS MADE	NUMBER OF CHILDREN
Less than 9 months	5
9-21 months	8
More than 21 months	13
Remained over test limit	3
Total	29

Progress made in 9 months on Gapadol test

Even over the two-month period that I monitored my program in Alberta, I can report successes in *motivation*, in the *variety* of reading and in the *number* of books read.

At the beginning of the program, the questionnaire investigating reading attitudes showed that 20 per cent of the class disliked reading and another 20 per cent were indifferent. At the end, none of them reported not liking reading and only 13 per cent were indifferent. The others had grown to like it. Those whose attitudes had changed for the better said this was a result of 'all the extra books in the class'. They hadn't liked reading before because they 'hadn't been able to find good books to read'.

As well as a change in students' own written responses, there were observable changes in student behavior. They were often seen reading before school began and at recesses. Some started visiting the town library voluntarily. They became increasingly better prepared for silent reading, and their interests expanded as a result of trying out the books that were available. Allowing time for free reading during the school day had made the difference. Once students experienced reading as a pleasure, they found many ways to read more.

Unfortunately some of the children were not changed by the program. Thirteen per cent could still not see the point of reading. But this was in a community where all but one class member owned television sets, 60 per cent had video recorders and 90 per cent had 'pay television'. Most of these children viewed reading as something that, in the words of one of them, 'filled in time when there was nothing good on television'.

The number of books read during the program increased dramatically. At the beginning of the program the class averaged about fifty books a month. At the end of a ten-week period average monthly reading had more than trebled. Of course, the amount of class time given to reading would account for much of this increase.

My evaluation revealed that the sharing process was a significant factor in the children's changed attitude to reading. The benefits of discussing in class what was being read are best exemplified by the following three anecdotes.

> One boy was a sports fanatic. He displayed negligible interest in print, contenting himself with browsing through magazines and comics . . . until the day that another child brought a paperback biography of Wayne Gretzky to school. Gretzky is the current Canadian ice hockey superstar, and plays for the local team, who are also reigning champions. Once the fan started reading the paperback there was no stopping him. Whereas he had been a mildly disruptive and restless influence during the early days in the program, not a sound came from him when he possessed the book. In fact he made it quite clear that he thought silent reading time should be extended.

In another instance I spotted a boy reading *War of the Worlds* by H. G. Wells, and asked him to tell the class about it. This prompted another child to bring Richard Burton's recording of the book to school the next day. I played the record over the next two days, and during that time the remaining three copies in the school library were borrowed by other class members. I hadn't been aware that this had happened until the school librarian remarked to me that he had a 'run on H. G. Wells'.

> My Canadian home had the Narnia series on its bookshelf. I took the set to school and left it on my desk, intending to read extracts aloud from it. But the books disappeared off my desk and were found with the nearest group. They read the lot. My placing the books on my desk had not been a deliberate ploy to create interest so I was delighted with the result, even if I had to find new reading-aloud material.

Stories like these are not unique to my class. Once children have been given a chance to choose and taste good books and time to read them, they are hungry for more.

The individualised reading program has succeeded in my classes beyond my greatest expectations in some aspects, and yet has not measured up in others. I have seen unexpected changes in children's confidence and independence as lifetime readers; but I have also been disappointed by some children not taking the opportunities that were offered. But through the joys and the disappointments the program has allowed me a framework for classroom reading with which I am very comfortable. It gives me a chance to share books that I love, to hear about books that please the children, and we all have plenty of opportunities to find out more about the treasury that is literature.

References _____

Berglind, R. and Johns, J. 'A Primer on USSR', *The Reading Teacher*, February 1983.

Hittleman, D. R. *Developing Reading: A Psycholinguistic Perspective*, Rand McNally, 1978.

Huck, C. *Children's Literature in the Elementary School*, Holt, Rinehart and Winston, 1976.

McCracken, R. and McCracken, M. 'Modeling is the key to Sustained Silent Reading', *The Reading Teacher* 31 (Jan. 1978), pp. 406–8.

Meek, M. *Learning to Read*, Bodley Head, 1982.

Miller, W. *Teaching Elementary Reading Today*, Holt, Rinehart and Winston, 1984.

Core Library, Level I, Ashton Scholastic, 1984.

Sloan, P. and Latham, R. *Teaching Reading is . . .*, Nelson, 1981.

Veatch, J. *Individualising Your Reading Program*, Putnam, 1959.

Beginning a literature-based program

Developing a program over a year   2

Helen Kerin

It took all of a year to develop my reading program so that all aspects of the language program were integrated, the reading program was individualised and reading activities were both purposeful and pleasurable.

My setting up of a literature-based reading program involved large changes to my timetable, a decision to incorporate language contracts for the children and the participation of parents.

From the beginning I saw reading as an integral part of the children's learning. I also believe that reading, writing, spelling and speaking are all closely linked and should be integrated in a language program. Further, I believe that children learn to read by reading and they learn best when reading is seen as an enjoyable task. For this to happen I believe it is essential for the classroom to have a positive atmosphere where the focus is on reading for real purposes.

Where to begin?

I set out to establish three things in the first few weeks of term with my years 3 and 4 children:

- [ ] a reading corner
- [ ] a changing class library
- [ ] a supportive classroom for reading

To do this I had to find out what the children's reading interests and abilities were. I began by planning the classroom. The room needed to be a comfortable and attractive place for the children. I set aside an area in the room for a reading corner. It was a large area separated from the rest of the room by a hanging piece of hessian. Some cushions helped to make the area a place to relax with a book. It took time for the children to learn how to use it properly, but after a few weeks it was comfortable, quiet and full of books.

At the beginning of the year I chose a bulk loan of over fifty books from the main school library. As the year progressed the children and I made the selection (a different group of children each time) and we always had a selection of fiction, non-fiction (theme books), picture books and novels. I was careful to change the books at least every two weeks. At times we added books from Ashton's Core Libraries or the School Libraries Branch, and books that children had brought from home. During the year we had a lot of discussion about selecting books either by the title, by reading a small section, by following personal recommendations from others in the class or by reading the publisher's blurb on the front or back cover. The children were free to take home any of the books from the classroom to read.

During the first two weeks of the school year, while I set out to develop a warm, positive environment, I also did a lot of whole-class activities. I decided to have reading for at least one hour each day and in this time I read aloud as many books as possible, and shared my enthusiasm for literature. Children then read individually and in the two weeks I managed to hear each of the twenty-seven children read and discuss books with them. I soon had a good idea of their different abilities and decided to carry out a deeper analysis with my less able readers, using a miscue analysis to help establish why and where they were experiencing difficulties. On the basis of what I learnt about my students I decided it was essential to extend the brighter children and build up the confidence of the slower readers.

I began to use Big Books with the slower readers, who soon experienced fun and success with these. I avoided basal readers and encouraged these children to select their own books for individual reading and noted that the less confident readers needed more continued help and guidance in selecting their books.

After the first weeks of school

As soon as I began to feel more confident about knowing the children's interests and ability levels, I added more components to the program. I decided to read aloud a class novel in serial form each day and do some work with reading non-fiction books.

I chose *Tales of a Fourth Grade Nothing* by Judy Blume as the first class novel to read aloud. This was a great success, and we discussed our own experiences with younger brothers and sisters. We read parts of stories from the overhead projector and predicted the endings to these stories in simple cloze activities where I encouraged children to guess words. We also did silent reading together for at least ten minutes daily, using books from the classroom library.

I introduced the children to non-fiction books in order to demonstrate that we read for various purposes. Before we read a non-fiction book we would make a list of 'What we know' and 'What we want to know' about a particular topic. The children then read non-fiction books to find out information.

At this time, I introduced the rule of thumb technique for measuring the difficulty of a book. For this technique, children place down one of four fingers and lastly a thumb for each difficult word on a page. If on a page of about 100 words the child has counted hard words on four fingers and a thumb (five hard words), then the book is probably too hard. Gradually, over the next few weeks, I began having a regular short book conference with each child.

By now the school year was well under way and at this time I realised that my reading program involved not only the work we did in the classroom, but also the reading the children did at home. For the program to be really successful I needed to inform and involve parents. I decided to hold an information night at school so that I could explain the program to parents and answer their questions. In preparation for the information night, I sent home a three-page letter, in which I outlined my beliefs about teaching language and ways parents might help. On the information night I stressed the idea that the children could do very well without basal readers and that they would be reading literature or 'real books' in my classroom.

Dear Parents,

I would like to take this opportunity to introduce you to my language program. I hope that we can develop a partnership which will greatly benefit your child.

I believe that you and I can play an important and valuable role in your child's progress. I am dividing this pamphlet into two main areas:

- MY BELIEFS AND ACTIONS IN THE CLASSROOM
- HOW YOU CAN HELP YOUR CHILD AT HOME

I will be holding an evening discussion for parents to explain more fully my language program.

My program consists of:

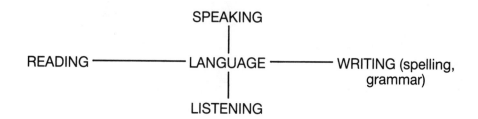

I feel that we cannot separate the four areas.

In my classroom I hope to create a warm, positive environment where children will develop confidence and will want to speak, read, write and listen.

Therefore I will:

- encourage the children to read and write every day and help them to understand the purpose of their work.
- offer a variety of experiences (e.g. excursions, sleep backs, camps) to enrich their language.
- encourage children to 'have a go' at spelling words and use 'look, cover, write, check' method of learning new words.
- encourage children to predict, guess and take risks when they are reading for meaning.
- use the 'process writing' approach with children where they choose their own topics, and give them the skills of editing, proof-reading and evaluating their own work.
- encourage individual progression in both reading and writing through personal discussion with each child.
- teach the conventions of language (i.e. grammar and punctuation) in a meaningful context.
- expose children to a variety of writing forms, e.g. poems, books, coupons, magazines, etc.
- encourage children to write for many different audiences.
- communicate regularly with you about your child's progress.

HOW CAN YOU HELP YOUR CHILD AT HOME?

TIME is often a worry — but I hope many of the suggestions below can be integrated into family life:-

- Encourage reading, writing, listening and speaking at home.
- Develop confidence and self esteem by encouragement and praise.
- Surround your child with relevant literature: books, magazines, comics, etc.
- Use books from school library, community library.
- Read aloud to your child as often as possible.
- Read along with your child.
- Discuss their stories with them.
- Listen to their ideas and answer their questions.
- Involve writing and reading in everyday activities:
  e.g. shopping lists
        newspaper
        telephone book
        street directories
        food labels
        using a 'note' system
        pin-up board
        television programs

- When you listen to your child read:
  — make it a positive, stress-free experience
  — when he/she stumbles on a word, tell the child the word
  — ask your child to retell the story in own words
  — realise the value of silent reading.
- Help your child with projects and homework in an encouraging way:
  — check homework (e.g. spelling words)
  — take your child to interesting places and discuss the trip with them.

Feel free to come along and chat with me about the progress of your child. I am usually available before and after school.

By mid-year

By June, the children were settled into a reading program where they selected books to read individually, and I was making sure that I read aloud to the children as often as possible. At this time I decided to increase the range of options children could undertake in the reading sessions. I arranged four options and the children moved into randomly selected groups for the following activities.

☐ *Listening post*: children listened to commercially produced tape recording of a story and completed a follow-up activity.

☐ *Book promotions*: children read a story and wrote an advertisement about the book, describing the main events and characters. They also drew or painted pictures to illustrate the book.

☐ *Silent reading*: children chose a book and read it quietly.

☐ *Group work with the teacher*: sometimes we worked on reading strategies such as predicting outcomes, retelling stories and poems or discussing the meaning of various stories. At times I used a technique named Predicted Substantiated Silent Discourse Reading, PSSDR (Sloan and Latham, 1981) in which I led the group in predicting what would happen in a story and then discussing whether these predictions were substantiated by what followed.

Here is a sample page from a reading journal

At this time we also began keeping reading journals. The children were invited to write opinions about some of the books they read. They did not have to write an opinion on every book read, but perhaps two out of every three books. The children kept a list of books read at the back of these journals.

The journal was a way for me to check what the children were reading, and their understanding of books.

Near the end of the year

In the third term I realised that certain aspects of my program needed to be modified. I now knew that for a successful literature-based program:

☐ reading must be enjoyable and any activities must be relevant and interesting;

☐ children do not need lots and lots of pieces of paper to fill in about the books they have read;

☐ children need to know exactly what is expected of them.

I needed to reorganise the program so that the students were clearer about what they had to do and valued any reading-related activity they did. I finally organised the program around a language contract which pulled together the different elements of the program in a manageable and individualised way.

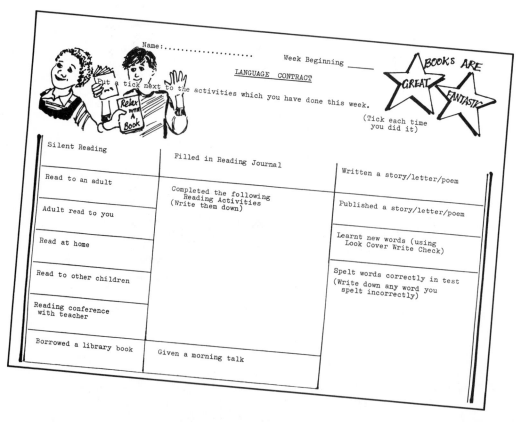

The language contract was given out each week and each item ticked as it was completed and the chosen activity written into the space provided. Each item on the language contract was clearly stated and easy to follow. Children were asked to read during the week to an adult, read at home, read to other children, and of course to read silently for a sustained period of time. They were also to have a book conference with me. During the individual book conference time I held a discussion with each child about the book or books read. I asked the children their opinion of stories and discussed with them their reading journal, and the reading activities they had completed. The children chose reading activities from a chart displayed in the classroom — shown in the photograph. The children were required to finish at least three of the listed activities each week.

BOOK ACTIVITIES

Things you can do when you have finished reading a book.

Do a brief book chat - telling us about the book.

Write a letter to a friend telling her/him about the book.

Write down main points of story.

Write a poem about the story.

Draw the main characters of the story.

Draw or paint a picture about the book.

Design a new cover for the book.

Hattie and the Fox

While the children worked on the language contract, I often conducted small or large group lessons on the following:

- ☐ cloze procedure for predicting from the text with Big Books and small books
- ☐ evaluating books according to story or the author's style of writing
- ☐ discussing book language or the language of a particular author
- ☐ reading for a purpose (non-fiction)
- ☐ poems
- ☐ choral reading
- ☐ predicting story outcomes or endings
- ☐ selecting books
- ☐ using Predicted Substantiated Silent Discourse Reading (PSSDR)
- ☐ asking open-ended questions to gauge children's responses to a book
- ☐ retelling stories

Integrating with other areas of the curriculum

I feel it is important to mention that as reading is not an isolated subject, integration with other aspects of language learning and other subjects occurs naturally in the classroom. Some examples of integration are:

☐ *Spelling* (see contract)   Words come from children's own writing and theme words.

☐ *Written language*   We have one hour of 'Conference Writing' a day. Children produce books, poems, letters and plays. They read these to younger children.

☐ *Oral language*   We have a lot of discussion about books, authors, poems and activities, during which everyone gets a chance to participate.

☐ *Social Studies*   Year 3/4 topics involve project work where many books are used for finding answers to questions.

☐ *Science*   Many topics are explored using various books.

☐ *Maths*   Children are encouraged to solve written problems, which involves a lot of reading, talking and writing.

Does the program work?

I have little faith in reading tests or their results, and while I did carry out a miscue analysis with children who found reading difficult, I believe that evaluation of a child's reading can best be done informally during everyday classroom interactions.

Informal means of evaluation include getting to know the children and their interests throughout the year. Observation of the children and their engagement in reading activities gives an indication of progress. Reading the reading journals reveals the number and type of books read, and allows one to check on the children's opinions about books. Daily informal discussion also reveals aspects of the children's reading development and their interests.

Book conferences are an excellent means of staying in touch with children's reading. We both discuss our opinions about books, the characters, the plot, the ending, and I usually ask the children to read a small extract of the book to gauge how well the book is matched to the child's ability. I always mark down the date and the main topic discussed at each conference.

A book conference

ANDREW

24/9 The snake that bites the sun
Good understanding of story
Could retell clearly and gave the
message of the story. Knew it
was an aboriginal girl.

29/9. Harry the Terrible Whatzit
Enjoyed the story could retell
the story. Sound understanding
of story. Did an opinion on story in
book journal. Read 3 pages aloud.

1/10 Aborigines
A little difficult at times, however,
he plodded through it because the
subject really interested him.
Language was sometimes difficult but
had an understanding of the story.
Could relate other stories about
aborigines

4/10 Pippi and the south seas.
Enjoyed story and was keen to
retell it. Read 3 pages aloud.
Did an opinion on story in book
journal. Is keen to read other "Pippi"
books.

10/10 Tikki-Tikki Tembo
Well read. sound understanding
of story. Could explain the message in story.

| ANDREW |
| JEFFREY |
| ANDREW P |
| BEN |
| DANIEL |
| DARRELL |
| IAN |
| COREY |
| BEN W |
| SONIA |
| TAMARA |
| RENAE |
| AMY |
| EMMA |
| NATALLE |
| MICHAEL |
| TOBY |
| CHARLES |
| ENID |
| STEVEN |
| JARROD |
| KIRSTEN |
| MEREDITH |
| BENNY |
| JAMES |
| EMMA S |

Record of book conferences

Evaluating a program also involves parents. Towards the end of the year I sent letters home to parents asking for their observations of reading habits and any changes they had seen at home. These helped me to find out which children need more encouragement in reading. All responses from the parents were very positive. Their comments reveal the positive changes to the children's attitudes towards reading and reveal the importance of communicating to parents about the ways we work in the classroom.

Julie has shown a marked increase in time spent reading at home. She has also been borrowing more books from the library + actually reading all through them, instead of taking them back unfinished. She has also start at home, g us about what She is readi reader at stories she

Sarah has always been a reader and enjoys telling us about the stories she has read. In the last couple of weeks she has been reading shorter stories to us rather than to herself. I would say there is increased interest, mainly in talking to us about the books she is reading at school and home. Dear Miss Keri

Dear Miss Ketur

Henry has shown an increased interest in reading books himself and his self-esteem appears to have risen considerably. Thank you.

Yes, Jeremy has shown an increased interest in books. As you are probably aware Trisha does have an interest in books. I am very pleased that you believe in the value of reading all types of material. I have endeavoured to direct Trishas interests in a wide variety of subjects from General Knowledge to plays. She has the ability to give a complete account of what she reads and very interest discusses the books with her. I am more and often ...." But I have the in fact, I can't keep her going, it's working!

your Keren

David has always liked reading books. But I have noticed lately that he does read more. He talks a lot about books that have been read at school. He enjoys reading harder books. He brings home different types of books from the library to read. (I feel these books are a little beyond his comprehension, but once I explain what I can, he seem satisfied).

Reference

Sloan, P. and Latham, R. *Teaching Reading is ...*, Nelson, 1981.

Beginning a literature-based program

A fresh start with a reception class   3

Pat Smith

After three years as a Language Consultant, I returned to the classroom eager to implement the ideas that I had been encouraging others to use. I was planning a program that would give a balanced classroom experience of reading, writing, speaking and listening, knowing that a wide range of language use would take place across these modes. Literature would be a major provider of content — of demonstrations of structure, of knowledge and ideas. I planned to allow plenty of time for book enjoyment. Having fun with books would be a top priority.

When Don Holdaway wrote about 'Literacy oriented pre-schoolers' (*The Foundations of Literacy*, 1979), he argued that the children ready to get on with the business of reading and writing were those with a background of book experience. I believe if children have missed out, there is nothing for it but for me to provide them with these experiences at school and also to keep on providing them for the others. If they come to reading early or late, they must be allowed to collect favorite books, which they will want read to them, or will read to themselves repeatedly; to see others reading and writing; to learn to be problem-solvers as they work with print. It is the life-lifting language of literature that will persuade children to have sustained, active encounters with books.

I know, too, that literature is important to young writers. Children need examples of a range of literature (including non-fiction) if their writing is to be stimulated and challenged. Otherwise it will be narrow in focus and arid in its use of language. If beginning writers reflect the styles of the books they are reading, it must follow that exploration and enjoyment of literature are vital for this intimate connection to develop further. I needed to time for
- ☐ reading aloud
- ☐ shared book experience
- ☐ language activities
- ☐ verse, song and chant
- ☐ silent reading
- ☐ a program that would offer real purposes for writing

Planning

I began by planning a classroom where there would be whole-class sharing of experiences, small-group work, and opportunities for varied individual interactions with books. I wanted to duplicate as closely as possible the conditions in which the children had learned to speak. I believe this is possible in large groups if whole-language demonstrations of reading are given and the individuals can take what they want from these and so learn at their own pace. Children also learn by asking questions of others, by being excited about what they know and explaining what they are learning. A positive self-image and the ability to form satisfying social relationships could be developed in such situations of co-operative learning. Because I wanted never to lose sight of the belief that really they teach themselves, and that I was there only to manage the process, I deliberately planned for this to occur by allocating time for my students to reflect upon their learning.

I introduced structures, knowing these could be withdrawn when the children no longer needed them. We would sometimes all become involved in some activity or another and it would seem pointless to stop simply because I had planned some other experience. I'd discuss this with the children and let them decide. Sometimes this happened with a small group or an individual, and I'd react in the same way. We fitted in excursions to the beach, theatre, zoo; walks in the bush; visitors; the principal sharing a great new book. These were not interruptions but part of a design to build a set of common experiences. I have continued to use the original structures as a basis for planning, but neither I nor the children have become constrained by them.

Setting up the physical environment so that learning would flourish was an important consideration. Provision needed to be made for play and talk, as well as quiet areas. Space was given to book shelves, a reading corner, a listening post, an open area in front of the easels for shared reading, an extensive 'dress-ups' wardrobe, the shop, cooking and house-corner. Where to put the sand trays and water play equipment was an easy decision: our new double classroom with shared cloakroom boasted vinyl floored wet areas with sinks and running water. The remainder of the classroom then became reading, writing or mathematics workshops, with all the materials stored for easy access. The children were able to function independently in a familiar environment and become active participants in their learning.

The various activity areas fulfilled many purposes. In the house-corner, the children developed the roles and language of adults. Dress-ups were used for role-playing and imaginative play; there was development of language which extended the children's knowledge of the world. I looked, listened and often took part myself. With the faith that I had created an environment which allowed language learning to occur, I became comfortable with a noisier classroom than before. This was a big adjustment for me to make, because I had always thought that a quiet classroom provided the best environment for maximum learning.

Enjoying literature

When books are published in an extra-large format, readers can enjoy literature together in a large group. At the same time they are engaging in a co-operative learning activity which builds confidence. Five years ago I read, and reread, Holdaway's *The Foundations of Literacy* (1979) and knew that these Big Books were for me. I went to school that year and used the activities outlined by the teachers who were involved in this study. I had co-opted husband, children and mother into helping me make similar Big Books and persuaded an understanding principal to let me have a go. I am now back in the same school where parents, teachers and children have made over a hundred Big Books. Top priority has also been given to buying the commercially produced Big Books as these have become available. I still believe that shared reading using large print should be the keystone of a reading program for beginning readers.

Shared books

The daily shared book experiences generally follow a set pattern. We always start with a particular author or illustrator. My Preps become part of a reading community as they develop and refine response and tastes through regular close looks at authors and illustrators. They seek favorite authors in the library. They carry on literary conversations. I overheard Luke, with *Amos and Boris* under his arm, tell Doug that he was going to the library to find another William Steig book to compare with this one. Another day, Tim and his friends persuaded the librarian that we needed all the Brian Wildsmith books in our room so that we could 'seriously examine the way he colors in'. Visitors are sometimes startled by the works of Wildsmith's faithful apprentices! The class have been great admirers of Quentin Blake since we read *Mr*

Magnolia at the beginning of the year, and are keen borrowers of his books, too.

Publicity about the Children's Book Awards gave us the idea of keeping a ladder of current favorites. I wrote the titles on card and pinned them in voting order. Often a group adjusted this to suit themselves or they asked me to write a new title to add to the list. Ann Coleridge's *The Friends of Emily Culpepper* was a constant front-runner all the year, but usually the rest of the list changed as we read new authors. The children also became very particular about retellings of fairy and folk tales. They responded with rapt attention to the storytellers who gave them stories to stretch their thinking, and demanded many repeat readings. Even titles assume importance. They prefer *Briar Rose* to *Sleeping Beauty* because as Lauren explained, 'It is a fitting name for a princess'.

Adjusting the ladder of favorites

My Preps have been able to meet some authors in person. Some of the children attended our district's Young Authors' Conference which had Morris Lurie as the guest author. These children were full of talk about what he had said to them. I had mistakenly believed that because he wrote for older children, the Preps would not get much from his talk about how he discovers his stories. Quite a few responded to his advice and wrote exaggerated stories about silly brothers! Lorraine Wilson called one day, and after she had talked about her writing, they asked wonderful questions. I remember that Richard fixed her with a reproachful eye and gently inquired, 'Why do you write such *short* stories?'. On each occasion both authors explained how they used real-life experiences as inspirations for their writing. These experiences with authors encouraged the children to read like writers, and so they have been more than ready to discuss the probability of characters and characters' actions.

We read and discussed many non-fiction books, too. Di Snowball's *The Chicken* was very popular. I told Di about this and the children were very excited when she sent them an autographed copy. Later in the day, I looked up to find some children organising a roster for borrowing by writing their names on the chalkboard. This worked so well that they have continued to do this for all their favorites. Their responses showed me that my class were developing and continually refining their taste in literature because of a program which encouraged this growing discernment.

I also learned how powerful personal connections with authors had been in forming these responses.

Reading aloud

Reading aloud is a very important part of the program. It was Bill Martin Jr, in his *Sounds of Language* series (1972+), who showed me ways of using literature to help children unlock print by having them become familiar through hearing, seeing in print, joining in and writing themselves, all kinds of sequence patterns in text structure. The old storytellers used these exaggerated clues of repetition, rhyming, cumulative and other predictable sequencing. Many of these tales have lasted to be used as written texts because of their memorability. *The House That Jack Built, The Old Woman and her Pig, The Three Pigs* and *The Fat Cat* are but a few of the stories showing patterns of cumulative writing which, once heard, can be stored for a lifetime of use. I found my children using story structures to unlock print as soon as we started talking about the patterns. There have been some exciting moments when the storyteller's secrets have been revealed. To think that in the past I used to believe that all these understandings were nothing to do with real reading! Now my children have taught me that I must read, read, read and give them a wealth of insights into text structure.

I believe that all the stories read and told to children are deposited in what Bill Martin refers to as 'linguistic storehouses', ready for future reference. I see this happening to my children when words or phrases they would not usually use appear in their writing. Dinah, writing about her performance in the school sports, stated that, 'I knew I would have to be *nimble* . . .' Marieta wrote about a storm and repeated 'It was dark indeed', on three occasions. When we are reading new books the children very quickly recognise any repetitive sequence and join in. They will comment that the folk tale 'The Greedy Fat Old Man' is like *The Fat Cat* because he eats everyone he meets until he is tricked into falling from the tree and bursts open and everyone gets out. I had barely started *Hairy Maclary from Donaldson's Dairy* when they launched into a discussion of the cumulative pattern and started speculating about the ending. Clinton in his story 'The Hungry Cow' used the cumulative sequence from *The Hungry Giant*. Knowing about Jack, Cinderella, witches, the Three Pigs, Little Red Riding Hood, Goldilocks and the gingerbread cottage, gave the children delight in the literary references in *The Jolly Postman*, by Janet and Allan Ahlberg.

Big Books

Then it is Big Book time. The children take pleasure in choosing the first one for the session. We often have the same book for days before a new favorite takes over. Sometimes there is a nostalgic return to an old favorite. I then introduce a new book or we take a further look at one that they don't know by heart. My children this year come in before school, or use any opportunity to role-play Big Book time! It is not unusual to find half the class reading to their friends, or even to an imaginary audience. I believe this happens because I show them how I unlock print successfully and support them as they do the same. The children are then confident and eager to engage in these demonstrations of themselves as readers.

An impromptu Big Book time

Chants and rhymes

I include chant, rhyme, dance, drama and music as part of the shared book session, because I believe that they are activities which have power to activate the learner. The oral transmission of culture demonstrates the success of this, and of corporate learning. Number rhymes and alphabet games are part of our culture, as are nursery rhymes. Playground chants, with their strong rhythm and beat, have always encouraged children to join in and have fun with language. This play develops familiarity and freedom in using language and I planned deliberately for this to happen.

I copied many poems, chants and rhymes in large print. These were used as wall charts and later bound into Big Books. All these expanded our stock so that I was able to offer the group new experiences in print every day. I found this to be a practical way of overcoming a shortage of large print when we started the program. I enjoyed finding new games, chants and poems to suit this class and so I shall always keep making more. We practised group readings for the class or for other classes. By preparing oral readings of poetry, and through improvised dance, music and drama, the children were able to demonstrate how well they had discovered meaning.

The children particularly enjoy the chants and games that rely upon the faithful observance of a steady beat and which make exciting, illustrated books. They had a page each to write and illustrate in the saga of Alice the camel and this meant the poor animal had to start with twenty-six humps!

> *Alice the camel has ( ) humps,*   (3 times)
>   *Go, Alice, go!*   (1½ beats hip swing)
>
> *Alice the camel has no humps,*   (3 times)
>   *Silly old Alice is a horse.*

The importance of maintaining an underlining beat became apparent when we had fun with the following chant:

> *Not last night but the night before,*
> *Three black cats came knocking at my door.*
> *I went out to let them in*
> *But they hit me on the head with the rolling pin.*

By gradually substituting body movements and/or sounds for words and phrases, the children learned that they had to keep the sound of the words in their head.

They explored the elements of musical language through

> *Order in the court!*
> *The judge is eating beans.*
> *His wife is in the bathtub*
> *Counting submarines!*

They said it LOUD and SOFT; HIGH and LOW; sounding BORED or EXCITED; QUICKLY or SLOWLY. I estimate that they now have a repertoire of fifty ways to say a chant!

Negotiating the curriculum

I wanted to give the children opportunities to negotiate their curriculum. To help them plan, I explained that there would be several activities for them to choose from every day. They decided that they would attend each activity at least once a week. Because I plan whole-language experiences it doesn't matter if the children miss an activity, but it was interesting to find that my Preps very quickly organised themselves to include the available options, if not in a week, then over a two-week span. I believe that this happened because they, young as they were, had made a commitment to their own learning. We took time to discuss what they had been doing and to affirm that they were active participants in determining what was happening to them.

In a week they might choose from:

☐ Two different listening post sessions (i.e. a repetition of a current Big Book or a story cassette). We have been buying sets of books from Ashton's Book Club and sets of Lion and Puffin paperbacks. These are stored in the library in plastic bags with home-made cassettes to supplement the available comercial recordings. The children are very enthusiastic about these sessions. Originally I had planned that these cassettes would offer interesting repetitions for the children who needed them, but everyone demands their turn to enjoy the storytelling.

☐ Art and drama activities where the children are encouraged to make group responses to literature.

☐ Whole-language follow-up activities which might be sequencing a story; matching sentences to a picture story; following instructions (e.g. cooking gingerbread men, making apple pies or doing a magic trick); practising and taping a story; devising variations on a story. Often parents and student teachers help with these activities.

There is another important component of our literature-based reading program. The school community had been used to the children bringing home readers to practise every night. I knew that a home reading program, where the emphasis would be more on books shared by the family, would be a welcome progression from this often boring or anxiety-fraught activity. The parents were invited to attend an in-service night before the children started school. I explained that I wanted our children to be readers from the first day. The children would be able to choose books which they really would want to read and would not be using sequential 'readers'.

We talked about how to share the stories. My Preps have been able to choose their books knowing that if they do take one which they can't read independently, their

A listening post group

A matching game

family read and enjoy it with them. When it became obvious that three children were missing out, I read with them, usually before school. I also talked to the parents and, because I was able to convince them that the main purpose of the program was for the family to enjoy reading together, they do often read with their children.

Some of the parents did worry in the beginning that the children would not be able to select their own books, but they soon saw that their fears were groundless. Children really do know what they can read! Sometimes a book is so special that a Prep will strive to read it. In October Amy had enjoyed listening to several readings of *Peace at Last* by Jill Murphy, and she borrowed it to take home. The next day she read the story to me with obvious enjoyment, confident in her ability to reconstruct the text meaningfully and self-correcting when her memory told her that something wasn't right. She stopped at the appropriate places to laugh and to explain that 'Mum thought that was funny', and 'Dad liked that'. A week later she returned with the same book and very determinedly set about decoding it. We worked together and twenty minutes later Amy, flushed with pride, announced 'I can read words now'. I am often aware of meaningful moments in the children's reading growth. In a program based on whole-language activities it is possible to give individuals your full attention because the others are self-directed. They aren't constantly seeking approval or asking what they will do next.

At the beginning of the year I encouraged the children to share their books with me because I wanted to gain an intimate knowledge of each child and their reading development. Then as the year went on, and I knew that they were aware of how to discuss a book, I decided to extend this. Now, when the children arrive in the morning they find a friend with whom to discuss the book. This is an embryonic readers' circle. I thought that this would be all that would happen this year, but some of the children have in fact begun to work as a group of five. They ask the same kinds of questions that I asked them and read a part of the story to illustrate a point.

Books are chosen from the attractive classroom library, which has a large stock of predictable stories including small versions of the Big Books. Funds provided by the Basic Literacy in Primary Schools program enabled us to build up this resource. This is a big change from the days when the classroom shelves were often the repository for discarded, dog-eared library books and Little Golden Books. The books are kept in plastic bins and on the shelves. The children seem to enjoy sorting them into various groupings. For example, they keep the books about dinosaurs, the Mr Men, the Dr Seuss and the Clifford books in separate boxes. These are not catalogued in the central library. I do running repairs but because most of them are paperbacks, we realise that these books, which are in constant use, can't be expected to have a very long shelf life.

We bulk-borrow from the school library and the municipal library, and the children keep track of these books too. There has been no trouble with missing books. I also organised a set of large pamphlet boxes in which the Preps store their current library books or perhaps ones they are reserving to read later. They are able to borrow individually from the library, of course. The most important outcome of all this would be that these children will feel at home in a library and continue the book-borrowing habit all their lives. They show every sign that this will be so!

We also have SQUIRT (Super-Quiet Un-Interrupted Reading Time). This is somewhat of a misnomer because Preps are noisy as they enjoy old favorites, interact with new books and share with friends. In the beginning, a few of the children were not really involved. I encouraged them to collect three or four books during the morning so that they wouldn't waste all SQUIRT. I also demonstrated telling a story from the illustrations and suggested that they could do the same. This helped them get started and it was not long before the influence of the shared book sessions became apparent. All the children, every day, are engrossed in enjoyment of their favourite books.

Engrossed in a book

Times for writing

From the first day of school, the Preps have been writers. Clipping some paper to the easel, I explained that I was going to write some news. I talked about keeping the message in my head and writing it down to read to others. To reassure some children who worried that they couldn't spell the words I said that no one else would be reading their writing, so spelling didn't matter. Most responded to this quite happily but it was necessary to support two anxious children for several weeks by refusing to spell words for them. I knew that if I provided spelling I was further demonstrating that they couldn't do it. They knew many letters and sounds, so I suggested they say the words slowly and write letters for the sounds. They would ask, 'Is that right?' and I would answer, 'Read it to me'. I would respond to the content. Once they really believed that this was the important aspect, spelling ceased to be an issue which interrupted their writing.

I make the children News Books by stapling paper between brightly colored cover card. Other loose paper is available but not popular for personal writing. The book form adds status to the writing. I write about my Preps in my diary while they are writing in their News Books. This is a valuable part of my record-keeping and I show them that personal writing is important to me. I store the finished books, and photocopy any changes as part of continuous assessment of their development as writers.

My writing demonstration continues to be an introductory segment before the children write themselves. I choose to write about personal and group experiences or coming events. I compose fiction and retell stories. I try for an interesting opening and a satisfying conclusion. I rewrite a boring sentence, or I change something that is not clear to the children. This demonstration happens every day so that the children can see a writer in action; choosing topics, rehearsing, reviewing and obtaining response.

I believed the reading/writing connections we were continuously making would empower the children to be writers. At the end of Term 1, it seemed difficult to assess the value of these demonstrations. Many children continued to draw, scribble, write letters or numbers. Travis and Christopher were concentrating on learning to write their names. I couldn't persuade them to write anything else! Six children were writing conventionally enough for me to read and another ten were using many conventional letters. I realised that I had more information than this. By reading back through my diary and looking through all their writing, and photocopying evidence, I was able to record exciting growth points for each child which showed that they were sensitive to the demonstrations. Twenty-six children were responding in as many ways.

We create as much time for sharing as possible. I share my writing with them and they share with their friends voluntarily in writing workshop time. At the finish of this session there is usually someone who wants to read a story to the class and ask for comments. Because I often ask them about their personal responses to their work and avoid saying 'That's good', the children handle this early version of an author's circle in a caring atmosphere. Someone always asks 'Why are you pleased with your writing?' The listeners sometimes want to clear up confusions in content or to ask for more detail. Quite often I notice that writers whose spelling is becoming conventional seem to concentrate on this and other aspects of their writing assume less importance. The questions seem to help them refocus on the story. They go back and add on information or put in a missing word.

I actively encourage my Preps to write about their own experiences and interests, and because we read so much exciting literature which reflects everyday happenings, they have, and will have, no problems with selecting topics. Voice sings, loud and clear, in their writing.

We gave the more dignified title 'writing workshop' to the writing session in Term 2. Many of the children had been making books and writing in them as a free-choice activity. I wanted to encourage this. I gave the children folders and organised plenty of paper for writing, cover paper, staplers and other necessities. I anticipated that fiction writing would start, but this didn't happen for months. I had read all kinds of books and demonstrated writing for different purposes so I didn't expect a surfeit of fiction, but the complete absence of it until near the middle of Term 3 was an astonishment to me. Instead the children wrote 'Books about . . .'. This writing is like an inventory with no order to it. It seems that narrative and expository writing are developing from these lists as my Preps learn to organise information and sequence events. Perhaps they need to do this before they tackle the more complex fiction-writing demonstrated to them in reading. A steady diet of fine literature will support their growth.

Ben is our dinosaur expert. He systematically borrowed every book on the subject and, with the help of parents who read and talked seemingly endlessly about dinosaurs, taught himself to read. He did not become a keen writer until late in second term, when he wrote many disorganised lists. Now he is writing a book about dinosaurs in which he is showing how much he has learned about organising information for an audience. He enjoys fiction stories about dinosaurs. He tells me that he will probably try writing one himself. The dinosaur books provided Ben with a purpose for learning to read very early in the year, and I believe they will continue to support his writing.

Some of the mothers helped each child publish a book using the Macintosh computer. I thought this would add to the Preps' view of themselves as authors. They are proud of these books but I find that they are quite happy to make their own by stapling some pages between some colored paper covers. My children seem to gain enough satisfaction from the writing and sharing times, and aren't too concerned about beautiful products.

In Term 3 we organised some cross-age tutoring which has been very successful. My Preps write to, and receive a letter from, a year 6 partner every week. They meet for about thirty minutes and read their letters and a story book to each other. The older children take care in selecting and practising their story, as do the Preps. The letters are written on proper notepaper and posted in envelopes. The conventions of letter-writing are observed. They write news, they ask questions and answer them. The letters of both age groups reflect personal knowledge and voice, in contrast to the letters produced in the old teacher-directed letter-writing sessions. They write letters to each other and to me quite often. They enjoy this purposeful reading and writing activity.

Written, two-way dialogues started because I wanted to encourage some of them to write more informatively. Of course all the children wanted a turn and when I found that most were keen to keep this fun going for twenty minutes, I decided to call for help. Luckily, the year 4 teacher was keen to give her children real purposes for using standard spelling and neat writing in first drafts. This interest in handwriting was caught by the Preps, and many of them began using lower case letters where before only a few had been doing so. They enjoy these written conversations which extend their thinking.

How it's working

The results of using literature as a base for the reading program are evident. Ken Goodman said, 'If you want a child to learn about cats and dogs then put him in a room with a thousand cats and a thousand dogs'. My Preps have been surrounded with wonderful books; they have had demonstrations that allowed them to learn; they have engaged in reading and writing because they have felt the need and they knew that they could. They all, without exception, regard themselves as successful readers and writers. Some of them will need more time, more stories read to them, more talk about how the reading process works, more shared book experiences, before they take off as independent readers. I know, because I am able to document so many growth points, that it won't be long before this happens.

The children are undeniably writers, and often write for the sheer enjoyment of it. Because literature has dominated their reading experience, and because real needs for writing have been presented to the children, they do writing of many kinds. It doesn't seem important in what genre they start, as long as we appreciate the role of real literature in early reading and writing.

References _____

Holdaway, Don *The Foundations of Literacy*, Ashton Scholastic, 1979.
Martin, Bill Jr *Sounds of Language* series, 2nd edn, Holt, Rinehart and Winston, 1972-74.

Beginning a literature-based program

A school changes its program   4

Shirley Yeates

The staff at our school were concerned that our children weren't really enjoying their reading. They had decided that the main reason was that the reading program at the school was based on progressing sequentially through basal readers, occasionally supplemented by class loans from the school library.

As Language Arts co-ordinator, R-7, I set out to support the staff in changing the program, recognising that we would have to take into account the very high proportion of ethnic and single-parent families in our school. Our experience was that neither of these sorts of families tended to have access to very much literature. I realised that for many students the basal reader might be the only book they had. I knew that much of their leisure time was spent watching television. My focus was to stimulate more interest in literature.

The children had accepted that readers were books from which they learnt to read, they were special *school* books. We had a record chart for each child, listing each graded reader, which was marked off as it was read by that child. This record was kept in a student record folder that progressed from class to class with the student. Some children were still trying to struggle through a graded reader that they *should have read* (according to its grading) a couple of years ago. This of course was turning them away from reading and also lowering their self-esteem.

Planning with the whole staff

I realised that our school's language policy would have to be modified, and that we would have to change the way we recorded children's reading progress. The first step was to consult with the principal. He gave his whole-hearted support. He had already started weeding out old dilapidated readers and disposing of ancient reading laboratories. He knew that there were more exciting, relevant publications available that were more in keeping with the children's experiences, interests and language.

The librarian and I realised that if our literature-based program was to get off the ground we would need to work closely together and pool all of our reading resources.

At our staff meeting, the idea to change the nature of our reading program was discussed and met with enthusiasm. Some concerns were:
- [ ] How would reading records be kept?
- [ ] Do we have enough material in the school to effectively implement a literature-based program?
- [ ] How will the parents react?

These questions were discussed at length and we came to these conclusions.

How shall we record?

It was suggested that each child keep a record of his or her reading on a sheet kept in the back of the book currently being read. These sheets would be signed by a teacher or parent and would be a record of the number and type of books read. They could be collected at the end of the year and passed on to the child's next teacher. Here is an example.

My Reading Record				David F
Title	Author	Page	Date	Signed
Sly old wardrobe	Southall	54	3/5	BH
"	"	93	11/5	BH
"	"	164	24/5	BH
Devil's Hill	Chavey	10	6/6	BH
"	"	98	18/6	BH

Another suggestion was for class teachers to keep a list of each child's reading. It was decided that each teacher would use the record-keeping method that best suited the particular classroom's program.

Enough books?

To gauge the quantities of books needed, and the program's effectiveness, the staff decided to trial the approach in four classes only to start with. Basal readers were to be included in the classroom literature, but there would be a greater emphasis on books from the library and on sharing Big Books.

What about the parents?

Some teachers were concerned that parents might object if their children were not taking home the expected 'readers'. One teacher reported having a difficult time with a parent when the children had been allowed to choose their own 'take home' books. The objection was to *Story Box* books (Rigby, 1984), which the mother considered were not really being read as the son didn't know all the words: 'He guesses most of the time', or 'looks at the pictures' were the main objections. Even though the teacher tried to explain that the important consideration was that Johnny was enjoying reading and using all cue systems (Goodman, 1968) the parent insisted that he have a 'proper reader'. The staff suggested a parent workshop to help avoid this problem.

We also decided to introduce the new approach to reading by working with themes. We thought that this would spread the literature available more evenly throughout the classrooms, with each having a different focus. The classroom teachers had different rationales in choosing the initial themes. Some related the theme to their Social Studies or Health topics already programmed, others chose to be guided by their students' interests.

These choices indicated the changing attitudes to reading: that other subject areas could be integrated with reading, and that reading could be related to *purpose*.

Two themes with a year 3 class

A year 3 class had been studying Australian animals and the teacher wanted to base the reading program on that theme. Together we sifted through the basal readers to find any which contained relevant material, and the librarian assisted us in choosing books with Australian animal content — fiction, non-fiction and poetry. The first lesson was to explain to the children about the new focus on reading.

First I questioned the class on why we need to be able to read, and gained responses such as:

☐ to get information
☐ to give us something to do
☐ to be able to read letters
☐ to get enjoyment

The next question was 'Who likes reading?' and most hands went up (possibly to please me). But of those who hadn't responded the consensus seemed to be

☐ because it's too hard
☐ because it's boring

but all said they liked listening to stories, which showed they weren't averse to literature. I then explained that the teacher and I were going to try to make their reading program more interesting.

The aspect of this introductory lesson that gained the most positive reaction was the news that they could choose their own books. Previously the children had been progressing sequentially through graded readers, so this innovation pleased them.

One of the *Kangaroo Creek Gang* Shared Readers (Methuen, 1981), titled *The Animals that Loved Reading*, was an excellent resource to introduce the theme. It contains ideas about the different aspects of reading for pleasure, and introduces the characters in the *Kangaroo Creek Gang* series as it tells their reading preferences. Silent reading time, which was already familiar to this class, is also mentioned in the story. Having already been introduced to the characters and the literary style of the series, the class was keen to begin reading the books. We then showed the class the range of the animal books we had collected and explained that any could be borrowed; and the children chose their books.

Before the reading began we discussed how records of the books read could be kept. The children chose to make their own little booklets during craft time and call them 'Books I Have Read About Australian Animals'. Inside the booklets they would record the title and author of each book and review those that they particularly enjoyed.

As part of Drama the class mimed animal movements. This developed into some children choosing to act out a story they had read. An excellent resource for this dramatisation is Hodgson, *The Australian Puppet Book* (1984), particularly if the accompanying animal puppets are also purchased. It has five sections:

1　Staging plays and puppet-making
2　Music and verse
3　Plays and stories
4　Australian legends
5　Quiz time

The book has simple language and a wealth of practical ideas with consideration given particularly to second-language learners. There are three different scripts which can be photocopied without infringing copyright. The class worked in three groups to produce the plays. If there were not enough characters for everyone in the group to have a part, more were created amid much discussion and decision-making. The songs in the book were learnt and sung at school assembly, with children using puppets to accompany the words.

The Kangaroo Creek Gang
The Animals That Loved Reading
Written by Terry Watt   Illustrated by Terry Roberts

As many Australian children love reading, so do some animals. That is, only special animals like the ones that live at Kangaroo Creek. The animals of Kangaroo Creek loved reading so much that they would set aside times in the day to read. They called this time Kangaroo Creek Silent Reading Time. Everyone agreed not to make a noise during that time. This way everyone could read silently without interruption.

1

Animal outlines used

My Grandma Lived in Gooligulch proved to be an excellent Big Book to share during the theme. It has superb illustrations of Australian wildlife which complement the text.

Story-writing developed around the Kangaroo Creek Gang, with each child choosing a character on which to base a story. Sheets of paper with an outline of each character were available for the finished writing. The stories were to be compiled into group booklets about further adventures of the Kangaroo Creek Gang. They were later shared with other classes.

Other titles that were particularly valuable for this theme are listed below.

Books found useful for the Australian animals theme

Axelson, S.	*Eucalyptus Christmas*, Hodder and Stoughton
Bose, G.	*My Grandma Lived in Gooligulch*, Nelson
Diestel-Fedderson, M.	*Tari's First Christmas*, Era
Fox, M.	*Possum Magic*, Omnibus
Gibbs, M.	*Snugglepot and Cuddlepie*, Angus & Robertson
Hewett, A.	*Kangaroo Joey Finds his Shadow*, Ashton Scholastic
Lawson, H.	*The Loaded Dog*, Angus & Robertson
Lofts, P.	*The Echidna and the Shade Tree*, Ashton Scholastic
Lupi-Bobf, F.	*Billabong Land*, Lester Townsend
Park, R.	*The Muddle-Headed Wombat*, Angus & Robertson
Thiele, C.	*Flip Flop and Tiger Snake*, Rigby
Thiele, C.	*Pinquo*, Rigby
Vaughan, M.	*Wombat Stew*, Ashton Scholastic
Wagner, J.	*The Bunyip of Berkeley Creek*, Penguin
Wall, D.	*Blinky Bill*, Angus & Robertson
Watt, T.	*The Kangaroo Creek Gang*, Shared Readers, Sets 1 and 2, Methuen
White, O.	*Super-roo of Mungalongaloo*, Penguin

The next theme developed in this particular class was food. The three-week program was developed along similar lines to the Australian animal theme. The steps followed can be listed roughly as:

1   an introductory activity (e.g. unpacking a picnic basket);
2   teacher introduce the books and each child chooses one to read;
3   relevant class activities (e.g. read together *Pancakes* nursery rhyme and the class makes pancakes using a large printed recipe);
4   children talk about books read (and share favorite recipes);
5   other related activities (e.g. cook spaghetti Bolognese after a student has read aloud *More Spaghetti I Say!* by R. Gelman).

Books for this theme were stored in a lunch basket, and cooking was added to the activities begun in the animal theme.

Books found useful for the cooking theme

From the Young Australia series, Nelson:
> *Red Jelly*
> *Porridge*
> *The Picnic*
> *A Recipe Book*
> *Food for Thought*
> *The Emperor's Oblong Pancake*
> *The Earthquake Cake*
> *Our International Tasting Tour*

From Reading Rigby, Rigby:
> *The Beater*

From Reading 360, Longman Cheshire:
> *My Lunch*
> *The Animals' Picnic*
> *Teachers Don't Eat Sausages*

From the Story Box series, Rigby:
> *The Monster's Party*
> *I Want an Icecream*

The Chocolate Cake
Who's Going to Lick the Bowl
The Hungry Monster
Yum and Yuk

Ahlberg, A.   *Mrs Wobble and the Waitress*, Penguin
Armitage, R. & D. *Ice Cream for Rosie*, Ashton Scholastic
Edwards, P.   *Simple Soup*, Miller Educational
Gelman, R.   *More Spaghetti I Say!* Ashton Scholastic
Kuratomi, C.   *Mr Bear and Apple Jam*, McDonald
Lindsay, N.   *The Magic Pudding*, Penguin
Mattingley, C.   *The Great Ballagindi Damper Bake*, Angus & Robertson
Morris, N.   *Charlie Waits for Tea*, Hodder and Stoughton
Ridyard, D.   *Fish Story*, Ashton Scholastic
Sage, A.   *The Ogre Banquet*, Benn
Smith, W.   *Elephant in the Kitchen*, Ashton Scholastic
Tallon, R.   *Fish Story*, Ashton Scholastic
Non-fiction
Davies, S. C.   *Food for Australians*, Rigby
                    Cooking — Making Things to Eat, Penguin
Freeman, N.   *Cook-Book for Kids*, Marshall Cavendish
Newman, N.   *Fun Food Feast*, Hutchinson
Sedgwick, V.   *My Learn to Cook Book*, Hamlyn

Other topics that were used which were particularly successful at the various year levels were:

years 1–2 Families, Pets	years 5–6 Fairy Tales, the Sea
years 4–5 Animals, Pirates	years 6–7 Adventure, Australia

Parent workshops

As expected, some teachers were asked by parents why their children were not taking home readers any more. This concerned staff members who did not have the time during lessons to explain why the changes to our reading curriculum had been made. The staff decided to have a parent workshop on Reading.

An invitation was sent home to all parents.

Dear Parents,
You are invited to attend a workshop about children's reading to be held in the Community Room on Wednesday, October 23rd at 1.30 p.m. – until 3 p.m.
Guest speaker will be Jenny Emery, a Language Arts Adviser.
Please try to come along to find out about current trends in Reading.
Shirley Yeates
(Language Arts Coordinator)

To add credibility to the discussion, the Regional Language Arts Adviser was a guest speaker. Parents tend to take more notice of theories presented by an 'expert' rather than a familiar class teacher.

During the workshop, parents considered how their children learnt to talk.

> Children undertake the complex task of learning to talk virtu-
> ally without any deliberate instruction . . . when children learn
> language, their focus is not primarily on language but on doing
> something else, making sense.   (ELIC, 1985)

And so it should be with reading. Children learn to read by making meaning of texts they are interested in. Basal readers are not the books that children are most interested in. They also often have stilted language which make the books difficult to read as well as giving little satisfaction to the reader.

Books from the *Story Box* series (Rigby, 1980+) were then shown to the parents as examples of stimulating stories with engaging plots and satisfying conclusions. The parents were given a chance to predict what would happen in the book *Mouse* from the series, and realised that the pictures as well as the repetition could support an inexperienced reader. Many admitted that they would often cover pictures when listening to their children read — to stop them from 'cheating'.

The workshop was successful in convincing most of the parents that learning to read should be easy and enjoyable, and that carefully selected literature was an important aspect of achieving this.

Cross-age tutoring

Cross-age tutoring was organised at this time for three main reasons.

☐ As a result of the new demands on the librarian's time she was unable to release teachers for sufficient non-contact time. Combining two classes at a time released more teachers for this purpose.

☐ The staff wanted more opportunities for the children to be exposed to literature; the tutoring provided a different form of exposure to books.

☐ One year 7 class had several children with behavior problems. Staff decided that these students might benefit by being given responsibility in interacting with younger children.

The class combinations were year 7 with year 3, year 4 with year 2, and year 4/5 with year 1/2. The librarian and I took these combinations in the library for one hour session a week.

At the beginning of each session, either the librarian or I read a story to the whole group and encouraged discussion about characters, theme and plot. As well as being an enjoyable book-sharing time, this provided a model for the children when they paired off with their own book.

When we first began these sessions we chose books around themes, such as ghosts, bears and fish. The books were placed in a central position and each pair would choose their book to share. After three weeks on a theme, the pairs would choose the book they wanted to write about. Their thoughts were recorded on the segments of an articulated shape. The shapes would be assembled with split pins to be displayed in the library or taken home.

The cross-age tutoring has developed from this sharing of books on themes to the older children helping the younger ones with a variety of activities:

☐ using the catalogue for particular topics, titles and authors:
☐ making posters to advertise a book
☐ designing different covers
☐ sharing home-made publications from writing sessions
☐ providing audiences for each others' drama work

Six months later

There is much more enthusiasm for reading. This is evident in the need to change classroom bulk loans more frequently, in more books being borrowed voluntarily from the library, a change from more non-fiction than fiction being borrowed to a preponderance of fiction, and in an increase in the number of books being read — as shown on the students' individual records. Choosing their own books is resulting in the children understanding and remembering more of what they read. The better readers are probably reading the same amount, but the reluctant readers are reading significantly more. Often the choice is a thin book with large print and plenty of pictures, but these students are reading, and as they read their self-confidence and their view of themselves as readers improve. The increased enthusiasm for reading has also meant that the school's supply of books is struggling to keep up with the students' demand. We will have to budget for more books.

There is also a noticeable improvement in children's style of writing. The children's writing is more fluent, the language more appropriate for written work, the stories are better structured, and the young writers are being more adventurous with the less familiar words. There is also experimenting with many forms of written language, and the writing is reflecting the topics and writing styles of the authors they are reading.

Some parents are not yet convinced that their children are reading and being helped to read when they bring home books that are easy, are obviously not from a reading scheme, or when they cannot read a book word perfect. We are planning more parent workshops and next year the parents will be sent letters to explain the Language Arts/Literature program. All the teachers who were in the pilot program are sure that they want to continue with the approach.

References _____

ELIC (Early Literacy Inservice Course) *Young Children Learn Language*, Education Department of South Australia, 1985

Goodman, K. 'The Psycholinguistic Nature of the Reading Process', in K. Goodman (ed.), *The Psycholinguistic Nature of the Reading Process*, Wayne State University Press, 1968

Hodgson, J. *The Australian Puppet Book*, Martin Educational, 1984

Huck, C. *Children's Literature in the Elementary Classroom*, Holt, Rinehart and Winston, 1979

The Kangaroo Creek Gang series, Methuen, 1981

The Story Box series, Rigby, 1984

Beginning a literature-based program

Converting to a literature-based reading program   5

Kathleen Graham

After several years of literature promotion through the school library, I was forced to recall the old adage, 'you can lead a horse to water but you can't make it drink'. Despite library displays of new materials and on various themes; quizzes, contests and games; storytelling and puppets; beanbags and cushions; book talks and discovery lessons, some children developed no thirst for reading. The solution had to be to extend the literature program into the classrooms. What hope had I with the children who were not 'turned on' by literature if, on the other hand, they were experiencing reading as a *lesson*; as a struggle to decode print; as a threatening 'round robin' where one's failings were made public; as a series of dull texts which bore little resemblance to any language experiences they had had; as an endless succession of books and levels with no end and little purpose; and as question-and-answer, right-or-wrong comprehension exercises in interminable laboratories! This is what reading meant to many of our students. Is it any wonder that they viewed it as a distasteful exercise to be avoided if at all possible?

My response to this was to work with three teachers for one exciting year to develop a literature-based approach to reading in their classrooms. I then transferred to another school where reading was taught along very traditional lines. I had now seen the rewards of using a literature-based approach and tasted success with our program, but here I was, back amongst basal readers, laboratories and children who were, in the main, uninterested low achievers as readers.

How then to change the situation? The teachers were professionals and they were conscientiously performing the teaching of reading with thoroughness and dedication in the way they had learnt it should be taught. Who was I to tell them they should do it otherwise?

My approach has been a somewhat oblique one, but, I feel, appropriate to the circumstances. As a teacher-librarian I am not in a position of authority. I therefore had two tasks — to encourage change from within people themselves and to establish my own credibility as a program innovator.

Preparing for change

For an initial period of nearly a year I simply talked to teachers about books and reading, informally and supportively. Although largely confined to a classroom, teachers usually welcome sharing their experiences with someone who shows an interest. Informal follow-up to chance remarks made by children is a wonderful way of opening doors. 'Lee was telling me about that book you read to them — it sounds as though it was a great success.' Or, 'I saw you reading *The BFG* with your class. The children seemed really rapt in the story'. Wherever I could I encouraged the good things that were already happening with literature in classrooms. I also made mild, unthreatening suggestions like, 'If they enjoyed that, you might like to go on with this title', or 'I would love to have a display using the follow-up you did on *Penny Pollard*'. I found out about teachers' interests and capitalised on these by suggesting books that they themselves would enjoy. I gave brief introductions to new books at staff meetings and displayed new additions to the library. I also involved teachers in the selection of new books, and lent special requests to them immediately, bypassing the usual long processing procedures. All this helped to establish a climate where children's literature could be seen as valid for everyone and a stimulating component of the curriculum.

This 'softening-up' process proceeded more rapidly when teachers were involved in children's library lessons. Beginning a book which will capture the children's interest is a good ploy — they will beseech their teacher to finish it in classroom time. Having an introductory literature-based program for the weeks leading up to Children's Book Week was another non-threatening way of introducing the idea of literature as the basis for a reading program. Mention was made of the term 'literature-based reading' and books on that approach (see References) were bought and promoted to staff.

Coming from an already active program in my previous school, this period of groundwork was somewhat frustrating but I felt it was essential not to rush things at a pace which could not be accepted.

Introducing the program

Having put this time into preparation, I then felt ready to present a program. First, of course, was the need for support from the principal. This was a useful exercise in personal development, for I needed to have some structure in mind in order to convince others of the value of the program. I have been fortunate in having principals who have encouraged staff to take curriculum initiatives.

I then approached the staff as a whole. In my current school, this meant I had approximately an hour and a half on a staff development day at the beginning of the school year. I firmly believe that effective curriculum change cannot occur unless there is an acceptance of the underlying philosophy, so I presented my own philosophy on the learning of reading, which is based on the following assumptions:
- that children learn by doing;
- that daily practice of reading will encourage fluency;
- that children are better motivated when they choose their reading material themselves;
- that a reading program should cater for each individual;
- that reading as a leisure-time pursuit should be encouraged;
- that children who are able to take risks, make predictions and self-correct are showing effective reading skills;
- that the teacher should act as *facilitator* of children's learning.

I was delighted to see this brought much nodding and agreeing amongst my peers. From this I went on to discuss the introduction and implementation of a literature-based program in my previous school. This established my credibility as a program innovator, but I emphasised that the program would be tailored to individual needs and styles. I then outlined how I would like to work in supporting teachers interested in such an approach to reading. Briefly, this was by:
- assisting teachers in drawing up their own programs;
- working alongside the teacher while the program was introduced to students;
- providing full support as a team teacher during the early stages of the program;
- providing reading materials from which children could select;
- gradually withdrawing from the classroom, but continuing to support when or as needed.

After a question period which indicated a high level of interest, the session concluded with an invitation to browse through a selection of books which would be used in the program. I asked that interested people see me to indicate if they would like to be involved, and stood back to watch and listen. To my amazement, over half the classroom teachers expressed a desire to be involved! Imagine my feelings — rapture that my preparations had borne such fruit, and admiration of my colleagues for their receptiveness to new ideas.

The program in the classroom

Initially, I worked with only one teacher, coming into the classroom for a session each day and reducing this time as the program became established, so that new classes could join. This restriction was necessitated by my ongoing commitments in the school library, but it meant that we all (librarian, teachers and children) learnt from each other as the program expanded.

To begin with, I offered the teacher background reading material. I consider Don Holdaway's *Foundations of Literacy* (1979) a 'must', and suggest other readings as support and extension. Then we together planned a program to suit the needs of the teacher. Most teachers have an initial problem with this, as the method involves relinquishing much of the responsibility for what is to occur to the student. From being controllers, they must change their role to that of facilitator and guide. Thinking through the rationale and expectations at this stage helps to produce a program that is based on current beliefs about how children learn. A mere grafting of new methodology onto old beliefs will be disastrous in the long-term management of the program; where there is a fundamental lack of understanding, any difficulties encountered will be 'solved' by reversion to previous methodology.

Procedures that the teacher and I agreed on for a class usually looked like the following:

☐ all children will read every day;

☐ each child shall read aloud to teacher regularly;

☐ children will select their own reading material;

☐ records will be kept on reading problems, successes and attitudes;

☐ teaching of specific skills will be done as problems are diagnosed;

☐ follow-up activities will be introduced from time to time to stimulate further interest and cross-fertilisation.

Our overall objectives were

☐ that the children should develop positive images of themselves as readers; and

☐ that the children should become self-monitoring readers who strive for meaning.

In planning the program, it is useful with some teachers to look at all the elements of their current program and see how these can be met by a literature-based approach. Thus, a typical program might have looked like this:

Children in five groups based on reading ages rotated through these activities each week.

Most teachers considered key elements to be comprehension exercises, oral reading and skills.

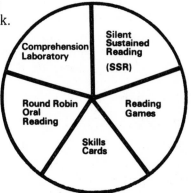

With a literature program, initial lessons generally follow this structure:

Years R-4		Years 5-7	
Big Book reading	10 min.	Big Book, or teacher reading aloud	10 min.
Book selection	5 min.		
Silent reading and conferencing	10 min.	Silent reading and conferencing	15 min.
Sharing of books	5 min.	Sharing of books read	5 min.

Expansion of these components will show how the key elements identified by teachers were incorporated, with all the added benefits of a literature-based approach.

Big Book reading

This introductory session involves teacher and children reading from a large-format book. Big Books are invaluable as familiarisation for poorer readers who subsequently are able to tackle the text on their own, either in the large or small format. As motivators, Big Books are supreme, engendering a sense of fun, excitement and participation. If the books are the classes' own creation, then ownership also is experienced. Skills can be developed using Big Books, by spending time on cloze techniques, blends, word endings, digraphs, phrasing, etc., depending on the text and the teacher's perception of students' needs.

Upper grades also benefit from Big Book activities. However, reading a longer book, or part of a book, is the more frequently used introductory segment with older classes. This enables the teacher to introduce authors and genres, to promote the skills of prediction, use of context and letter cues, and to model an enthusiasm for reading and literature, which in itself will be vital in the success of the program.

Silent sustained reading

During this segment, all children will be engaged in silent reading. To begin with, this is for a short time, but it will be extended as the children develop in their capacity to read independently and to be self-directed.

Expectations must first be clearly defined as to what will happen during the SSR period. I expect children to select a book or books which will occupy them for the entire period, so that there will be a minimum of movement. Children are expected to read quietly and independently and generally to complete the book they select, although of course allowance is made for personal dislikes if they occur. Early in the program we discuss book selection techniques, so that children are able to choose books they are likely to enjoy and to read with success.

Initially, the teacher will also read during this time, to present a model. We begin conferencing after a period of a week and use the SSR time, largely as a matter of expediency — there is only so much time in the daily timetable. This period should be used by the teacher wholly for interaction with children and their reading.

The reading conference

This can be for an individual or a group, but I favor the individual approach for its immediacy and intimacy. Initially, conferences are time-consuming while the teacher forms an assessment of each child's interests, strengths, weaknesses and needs, and establishes a good relationship with the child. In our program, the class teacher

and I jointly conference in the early stages. This enables me to model conference procedure, to otherwise support the teacher in a new approach and it allows for all children to feel involved from the outset.

Joint conferencing in class

Steps in a Conference

1. **Rapport:** Make sure the child is at ease by some friendly, welcoming comment, or question.

2. **Sharing:** Listen as the child tells something about his response to the book he wishes to talk about. Discuss any related activity he may be pursuing.

3. **Question:** Ask one or two searching, general questions concerning the theme of the book, the author's message or point of view, or the nature of the characters.

4. **Oral reading:** Listen to the child read a short passage he has selected to share with you.

5. **Records:** Check the child's *Reading Log* and make appropriate entries in your *Conference Log* concerning progress, interests, and problems.

6. **Encourage and Guide:** Discuss plans for the future. Offer suggestions about selections of books. Set practice exercises where necessary. Suggest joining a group for special skills instruction where you see that a number of children display a similar need.

In lower grades, I like to move quietly round the room to have conferences, but older children respond better to the privacy of coming to a removed area.

During the conference, a running record is kept. I offer teachers a checklist as an initial guide. This alerts them to diagnosis of attitudes, comprehension, oral reading and decoding skills which were a stated requirement of their reading programs. Because this record fragments reading skills, it is only useful in the early stages of the new program.

In addition, we discuss conference techniques — how to encourage children to think about their reading and use contextual and semantic clues; how to accept errors if in context; when and how to correct errors if they occur; how to encourage risk-taking and esteem for themselves as readers. In some classes, especially lower grades, school assistants or parents assist with conferencing so that children can be listened to more frequently, and they also must be briefed on conference techniques. The following guidelines are taken from Holdaway, *Independence in Reading* (2nd edn, 1980), p. 56.

READING CONFERENCE RECORD

Name of student_____

Name of book _____ Date _____

How well child enjoyed this book: Very well___ Some___ Not very well___
Approximate level _____

Appropriateness of child's selection: Good___ Too easy___ Too hard___

COMPREHENSION: General understanding of book: Good___ Fair___ Poor___

	Very good	Good	Fair	Poor
−Unaided recall				
−Accuracy of recall				
−Recognition of main ideas				
−Recall in questions				
−Inferences and evaluation				

ORAL READING: Fluency: Good___ Fair___ Poor___
Rate: Good___ Too slow___ Too fast___

___Word-by-word reading
___Poor phrasing
___Lacks good sight vocabulary
___Reversals: letter/word/phrase
___Frequent hesitations
___Guesses at unknown words
___Gross mispronunciations
___Substitutions
___Needs prompting on words
___Ignores errors
___Ignores punctuation
___Repetitions: words/phrases
___Omissions: sounds/words
___Additions: sounds/words
___Makes errors on easy words
___Confuses similar-looking words
___Loses place frequently
___Self-corrects many mistakes and word errors

WORD RECOGNITION: General accuracy of word perception: Good___ Fair___ Poor___

Needs help in:
___Development of adequate sight vocabulary
___Rapid recognition of common word parts
___Developing skill in attacking unfamiliar words
___Sounding through words effectively
___Avoiding careless errors on easy words
___Noting the absolutely essential distinguishing features and details of words
___Avoiding locational errors: beginning/middle/end
___Recognizing syllables and larger units
___Using effective visual analysis of words
___Auditory analysis of words
___Sounds of consonants/consonant clusters
___Sounds of vowels/vowel combinations
___Variant sounds of consonants/vowels
___Eye movements/eye-voice span
___Applying phonemic and structural principles

Weak in:
___Context clues
___Configuration clues
___Phonemic analysis
___Structural analysis
___Perceiving larger units in words
___Accurate, rapid word recognition

SUMMARY:

RECOMMENDATIONS:

We maintain a record sheet for each individual in a class. Each conference date is noted, with a comment on the child's progress as well as any action being taken or recommended. The title being read is also useful as an indicator of progress and application. For the teacher, the rewards of this type of record are tremendous, as an exact and individualised record is available which includes all the immeasurable aspects which standardised tests fail to identify.

Example from a conference record (year 7)

Sharing of books

The SSR session concludes with a sharing time. This frequently is an unstructured session when children read together in pairs, share Big Books or tell another person about the book they have read. It can be varied with a more formal approach when individuals are invited to share a book with the class or to display book-based activities such as drawings, constructions, their own writing or plays. This sharing time is very important, especially initially, and younger children will like to have this activity every day. It is an exciting segment for the children and for the teacher, as it sets the climate for a literature-centred classroom. I cannot describe the thrill of watching a class of formerly reluctant and uninterested readers chattering, enthusing and laughing over their books. Undirected, they spontaneously share and delight in their books with an enthusiasm which I consider alone vindicates the entire program.

Reading at home

As I believe that reading is learnt by reading and that it should be encouraged as a leisure-time activity, I expect children to read at home. It is important that books be read intensively over a short period of time. It is only when reading is consistent that children will become absorbed by the story, and it is this deep and complete involvement of the reader which is the essence of really satisfying reading. Sporadic reading will produce readers able to decode but will not develop higher-order skills or a genuine love of reading.

To minimise loss of books, the borrowing must be recorded in some way. This can be as simple as shifting a stick with the child's name on it from one jar to another, upon the borrowing and return of a book.

Children's records

Once children are reading longer books, I like them to keep records of their reading. This not only provides a check on how the program is going, but commits the child to the book selected and also gives each child a dossier of his or her reading experiences. The log may be simply entries on a wall chart or additions to a 'bookworm', or it may be a notebook in which key data are recorded. We have found that if record-keeping requirements are too exacting, however, it becomes such a chore that it defeats the purpose and teachers who have commenced with such intentions have soon let them lapse.

Maintaining these 'logs' becomes a source of pride to the children. They are visible proof of their success as readers, and it is the experience of success which is a cornerstone of the program.

Developing the program

We have found this simple program structure is sufficient for an introduction. Although the teacher may feel a loss of control at first, in fact the program demands a high degree of underlying structure if it is to succeed, and these details occupy quite a deal of time initially, until a routine is established and working. Once expectations are established and teacher and children are operating comfortably, the program can be extended in a number of ways.

The **Big Book segment** can be varied with many activities. The teacher can discuss a book he/she has read, and offer it to interested children; children can promote books they have read; longer novels can be read in instalments. Reading aloud is invaluable for exposing children to the structures of written, as opposed to oral language, knowledge of which assists children in their own reading. We have found Bill Martin's *Sounds of Language* (1972+) books a useful source of material for this purpose.

Teachers of upper grades have found that their reading-aloud time has had to be extended in response to the children's demands. One year 7 teacher has read at least a dozen novels to her delighted class.

Other activities can be the sharing of children's follow-up activities from their reading, book 'auctions', film or video segments on books or authors, or simply an injection of a quantity of new material. By offering a variety of experience, interest is maintained.

Conference sessions gradually change in character as the program develops. With younger children, the emphasis changes from diagnosis to helping children develop as readers. This involves encouraging the use of context clues, cloze techniques and making predictions. As these skills develop, the redundancy of comprehension exercises becomes more apparent.

In upper grades, conferences with those children who have had limited success in becoming readers are a time to develop their skills. I have worked with children in year 7 who still lacked an adequate basic sight vocabulary; who 'read' by rushing through texts at breakneck speed, garbling unknown words in order to conceal poor skills, with absolutely no conception of meaning — a technique developed as a survival mechanism in round robin situations; and who made wild guesses at unknown words with no reference to syntactic or semantic clues. In every class of upper primary children there have been some children who still did not have power over their reading, yet who were products of English-speaking homes and had been six or seven years in school. These children need special support in provision of appropriate materials and much encouragement. Many display surprising gaps in their reading skills, which are readily diagnosed and can be addressed effectively in the relaxed and supportive conference atmosphere. When extra staff are available, they are used to ensure that poorer readers receive additional conferencing, help with book selection and specific reading problems and with all-important feedback about their development as readers.

The conference session not only allows for decoding skills to be developed, but allows for developing comprehension of a much higher order than the exercises of old. Children can be encouraged to predict, to hypothesise, to make judgements and analyses. More able readers can be further extended during these sessions to develop critical appreciation of the books read and to consider the underlying themes of the story. These children are rarely adequately catered for in conventional reading programs yet, like the poorer readers, they benefit from encouragement and from having a responsive listener.

Book sharing sessions can be extended in many ways. Don Holdaway (1980) suggests a huge variety of activities to follow on from completion of a book, and there are many other books with literature extension ideas. These follow-up activities provide opportunity to extend the program into other areas of the curriculum. Writing is a natural extension of reading, and follow-up may include children writing alternative endings to stories, writing and performing plays, or writing advertisements for

Class-made Big Books are very popular

books, to name a few. Apart from the frequent sharing periods, however, most classes in which I have worked have preferred occasional follow-ups, rather than regular ones. We have found these should be natural outgrowths or periodic interest bursts, rather than regular or set tasks. We all know from experience what analysing a book to death has done for us — let's not bring that into primary schools! Teachers who fall into the trap of setting regular follow-up tasks are generally experiencing doubts about the relinquishing of control.

It is this session which has produced visible proof in our classrooms of the emphasis that is placed on the literature programs. Displays have included Book of the Week features, children's writing, hanging displays of children's book-related activities, 1000 paper cranes, reading corners, and most conspicuously, books on desk tops! All this helps to maintain reading as a focus of interest, and reinforces children's concepts of themselves as readers.

Evaluation

Once the program was successfully established in several classrooms, I felt it was time to report to the staff on our progress. Evaluation took several forms. All teachers had tested children on a Holborn Reading Test at the beginning of the year, so this test was re-administered. Although there were no control groups tested, comparison could be made with children's capabilities as measured before the program began. Tests showed most children improving to levels in excess of their chronological age, whereas the majority had previously shown a steadily widening shortfall. A few had recorded astonishing scores of up to four years improvement in reading age in only six months on the program. These tests do measure only a small range of the skills which make up 'reading', but nonetheless they were most encouraging.

Evaluation included observations of children's use of the library. We found this to be far more purposeful and self-directed for all participating classes, with children borrowing more frequently and in larger quantities than in any of the non-participating classes — very often taking two novels at once so that they could have one to go on with or 'one for home and one for school'. Children's interest in reading was further evidenced by the much higher rate of book purchasing through the school-run book 'club' by children in participating classes.

Conferences provided for informal evaluation, and all teachers felt children were making good progress with interest in reading soaring in all classes and skills being transferred to other curriculum areas. Parents' remarks showed children were reading more at home.

Problems met

As time has gone by, there have been some problems to address. The success of the program does rest upon the commitment and enthusiasm of the teacher. It demands an understanding of process learning and an awareness of the benefits accruing from children exercising choice and responsibility for their own learning. Without this, the program carries the risk of teachers throwing structure to the winds and using reading as a 'busy time'; but this should not occur with proper in-servicing. Some have found the problems of slow learners a threat and have tended to retreat to basal readers, with their measurable results. These children need extra encouragement and assistance, for they are the very ones who should not be discouraged from reading and who will benefit enormously from having highly motivating material.

My role, as classes become established, has been to gradually withdraw from regular conferencing, joining the class once or twice a week, to do extensive work with the 'problem' readers. These children relish the extra attention and are growing in confidence and enthusiasm as their skills develop.

Specific problems may arise with regard to particular children or classroom management, but my close involvement with the classes has helped in working through these very quickly. With some children we have had to try a whole range of strategies, but so far we have not had to say of any that 'this is one who will not improve through this approach'. Our most resistant reader to date, a year 4 child, responded dramatically when we realised that he wanted thick-looking books to read, rather than the short easy stories which identified him as a failure. He now visits the library daily after school to borrow, in his words, 'a thick book at my level'!

For the future

I anticipate that most teachers will wish to become involved, judging by the interest expressed so far. Whether or not this becomes a whole-school program remains to be seen. I have seen exciting results where a whole school has adopted this approach, but I would prefer to see this occur only by consensus. Currently, a sub-committee is working on a school reading policy in the light of current theories and methodologies. This is involving the whole staff at each stage, and a policy is evolving which looks very exciting in its implications for children's learning and teacher actions.

I shall continue to offer my support in the classroom for those who are embarking on the program or who may be experiencing difficulties with individuals or with maintaining momentum. Working alongside teachers has meant we iron out any difficulties as they occur. It has also meant that we share the successes, and I feel that this, as much as anything, has helped to make the results so positive. Not only is enthusiasm infectious, but teachers deserve to be listened to and commended when their practices bring about such exciting results in children's learning. Initially, moral support and sharing helps smooth the uncertainty and doubts which often accompany a change in curriculum.

For me as librarian, the continuance of the program offers challenges. Already we are seeing changes in the profile of reading in the school. The year 6 children involved in the program are reading books which previously I would have seen few year 7s tackling and our year 3s are moving into the levels our year 5s found comfortable at the beginning of the year. Providing a variety of reading material is a huge task. This year we put over 800 titles into the boxed sets of books and with expected expansion we will need to double this number. Imagine the wealth of experience these children will have had by the time they leave primary school!

References

Hill, Susan *Books Alive! Using Literature in the Classroom*, Nelson, 1986.
Holdaway, Don *The Foundations of Literacy*, Ashton Scholastic, 1979.
Holdaway, Don *Independence in Reading*, 2nd edn, Ashton Scholastic, 1980.
Martin, Bill Jr and Brogan, Peggy *Bill Martin's Instant Readers: Teachers' Guide*, Holt, Rinehart and Winston, 1967.
Pulvertaft, Ann *Let's Breed Readers*, Ashton Scholastic, 1982.
Sloan, Peter and Latham, Ross *Teaching Reading is ...*, Nelson, 1981.

Programs with a special focus

A reading/writing program from the library 6

Meredith Kennedy

Children can benefit when teachers combine ideas and resources. This program evolved as a joint venture between myself — a teacher-librarian frustrated by minimal interaction with young readers — and a year 3 class teacher, Jill Truelove, who wanted to try out a new literature-based approach to teaching reading. With enthusiasm, we decided what our roles would be, implemented them and contemplated improvements for future programs of this nature.

In the beginning we visited a nearby school to see a successful literature-based reading/writing program in action, and also read books for ideas. Two in particular, *Towards a Reading-Writing Classroom* by Butler and Turbill (1984) and *Literacy through Literature* by Johnson and Louis (1985) were most helpful. We had frequent discussions about the school's rather rigid timetable, the mixed abilities of the children, previous attempts at similar schemes and the jobs and roles each of us would fill. Using each other as sounding boards was most valuable. We certainly did not rush to begin until we had thought through all areas and made careful preparations.

We agreed that a positive, enthusiastic attitude was of great importance in all we did with the children. This was easy as we felt confident working together. Between us we would help provide the children with:
- ☐ a good supply of appropriate books;
- ☐ purposes for their activities;
- ☐ models and demonstrations of what could be achieved;
- ☐ help in organisation of time;
- ☐ ideas to stimulate their thinking;
- ☐ encouragement and assistance of individuals.

My particular responsibilities each week were to provide easy access to suitable books with tantalising introductions and thought-providing ideas for talking and particularly for writing about books. We thought that literature would present good experiences or stimulus for children to use as starting points in their own writing. We wanted to explore the many techniques authors use in their writing. We also wanted to encourage written responses to the books the children read, as writing provides a chance to read, think through and refine responses to a book, whereas an oral discussion, being spontaneous and often 'off the top of the head', does not always demand a great deal of thinking from the reader.

The teacher was very concerned to monitor each child's work and to divide her time fairly between individuals. As evaluating the effectiveness of the program was most important, we decided to critically monitor the program throughout.

As a start we decided to gauge the children's reading interests with a reading interest inventory we devised.

We also decided to compare the children's attitude to reading before and after the program with the Heatherington Primary Attitude Scale (Alexander and Filler, 1976). However, we found this attitude scale was of limited value as we actually learned more from observing and interviewing the children. At the conclusion of the program we gave the Schonell Word Identification test, as this test had been given earlier in the year, and we wanted to compare the two results. The results of this test

PERSONAL QUESTIONNAIRE
NAME   AGE   DATE
1 I have .... brothers and .... sisters.
They are ...., ..., ..., ..., ..., ..., years old.
We like doing these things together ....
....
2 My father and I like to ....
My mother and I like to ....
I help at home by ....
3 After school and at weekends I ....
....
4 I have a pet ...., and ....
I would like to have a pet ....
5 I have travelled by bus, ☐ car, ☐ airplane, ☐ boat, ☐ train, ☐ bicycle, ☐
pony, ☐
I have visited a circus, ☐ zoo, ☐ farm ☐ hotel, ☐ airport, ☐ ...., ...
6 My hobby is .... and ....
7 My favourite T.V. programmes are ....,
......................................, and ....
8 I like to read about ....
The best book I ever read was ....
9 If I could have 3 wishes, I would wish:
1. ....
2. ....
3. ....
10 I read books at school, ☐ at home, ☐ ...., ...
11 I like to read because ....
....
Sometimes I don't like reading when ....
....
12 I enjoy writing because ....
....
Sometimes I don't like writing when ....
....

A reading interest inventory

similarly did not provide as much information as the informal procedures of observation and interview.

Organising materials

I selected a bulk loan of books from the library, based partly on information from the reading interest inventory. I selected adventure stories in response to the children's interests and made sure there was a range of books for children with different reading abilities, plus a selection of books from other fiction genres and some non-fiction.

We then developed a borrowing system for the classroom, using a separate 12 cm × 12 cm card for each book. These cards were kept in a file box in the classroom in alphabetical order by title. When borrowing a book, a child would find the title card in the file then fill out his or her name and the date the book was borrowed. When the book was returned the date was noted by the child. This was an excellent way of providing children with practice in library skills, and it gave us the opportunity to check the popularity of each book and the time the children were taking to read the books. Regular checks of this file also showed us what books to weed out.

LIST OF BOOKS I HAVE READ.

NAME _____

	AUTHOR	DATE
Who's a clever girl, then?	Impey	15.9.85
The B.F.G	Dahl	18.9.85
Bernice knows best	Dann	21.9.85
Imp	Darke	24.9.85
Doctor De Soto	Steig	30.9.85
The man who didn't	Kraslasky	
Peter and the wolf	Prokofiev	2.10.85
Mog in the dark	Kerr	3.10.85
Are you there, Bear	Maris	8.10.85
Jack and the beanstalk	Ross	10.10.85
Dorrie and the weather	coobs	12:10.85
Box Too big	keller	13.10.85
Meg and Mog	Nicoll	14.10.85
Tis your turn, Robertx Roger	Greiz	
Mrs. Pepperpot to the Rescue		
Dorrie and the magic elix		
Dorrie and the hunter house		

New Book Contract

Book Title: It's your turn Roger.
Author: Susanna Gretz.
Book started: 15.11.85
Book finished: 15.11.85
Opinion of book I liked the bit where the family, on the 3rd floor don't even have a table and for tea they have roots and snails.

Oral Reading 2 pages read 15.11.85 J.J.Peale signed.

Activity selected...story

Each child was then given a lined exercise book to use in the program. We fastened sheets at the back of these for the children to record the books they had read, and contract forms were stapled into them when children completed their contracts. We experimented with different kinds of contracts and decided to use a very simple format with plenty of space for individual written response. Fulfilling the contracts was the basic requirement of the program. For children who needed lots of guidance we used the contracts simply to ensure that the children were reading and writing about books. However, some children negotiated with us to undertake different kinds of writing activities based on the ideas generated in the literature sessions.

During each session the children met with the teacher or myself to talk about the particular book they had read and their written responses. We also enlisted the help of the teacher aide and several parents to help with the conferences, as time seemed to run out for the many individual conferences. We put up a wall chart for children to pin their names when they were ready for a conference.

Planning the literature sessions

I decided to organise the weekly sessions into three main parts:

☐ promoting a number of books;
☐ modelling specific ideas children could use in writing;
☐ conferencing with individual children about their reading and writing.

When selecting books to promote I tried to match them with the children's interests and reading abilities. To stimulate written response, I printed ideas for writing activities on small yellow cards attached to the front of the books, and I then modelled these ideas on the blackboard or with specially designed activity sheets. The children were free to take up these ideas if they chose, or complete a contract, or engage in some more general activities suggested on a wall chart — for example they could 'make a poster telling others about the book' or 'write to a character in the book'.

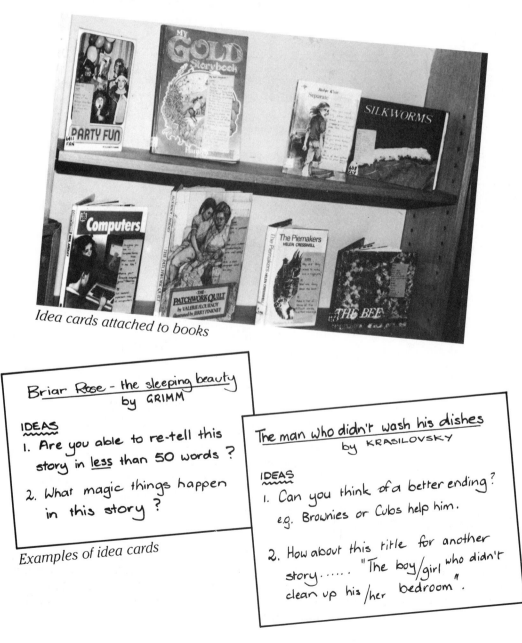

Idea cards attached to books

Briar Rose - the sleeping beauty
by GRIMM

IDEAS
1. Are you able to re-tell this story in less than 50 words?

2. What magic things happen in this story?

Examples of idea cards

The man who didn't wash his dishes
by KRASILOVSKY

IDEAS
1. Can you think of a better ending?
   e.g. Brownies or Cubs help him.

2. How about this title for another story...... "The boy/girl who didn't clean up his/her bedroom".

For some time I also wrote on larger cards a synopsis of the plot, character information, theme, tone, setting, humor, points of interest and an interesting question to ask a reader of that book in a conference. These were intended for Jill and myself, but we found we did not use them as it was not too difficult to devise questions during conferences. However, we thought the plot synopsis cards would be essential if using a similar program in years 5, 6 or 7, where the teacher or librarian needs to know the details of the book to hold an in-depth conversation with a reader. As an alternative to reading all the books, teachers could make use of generic questions to help in their discussions (see Butler and Turbill, 1984, pp. 51, 52). Reading books and making these information cards are time-consuming, but, may be well worth it later, especially years later! I had hoped to quickly build up plot synopsis cards for the class 'library' of up to 100 books. (I may do this next time.)

> **Thingnapped**   by **KLEIN, R.**
>
> Out of jealousy and spite, spoilt Stephanie Strobe kidnaps Thing, a friendly stegosaurus, from his loving owner, Emily Forbes. While a prisoner in Stephanie's bathroom, Thing shrinks from lack of food and escapes.
> Mrs Strobe finally stands up to her daughter's selfish demands and Thing is found in a bin in the park and returns home.
> Q. 1. Just how nasty was Stephanie?
> Q. 2. How did Thing suffer when he was kidnapped?

An example of a plot synopsis card

The literature sessions

When our initial organisation of books for the program and the form of the sessions were planned, we decided to go into action, keeping in mind that the program would probably change as we monitored the children's reactions and responses. I planned a session to introduce the program, then sessions in which we would try out different written forms in response to various books.

Session 1: introduction

I introduced the new system for borrowing books from the class bulk loan and then showed several of the 'all-time favorite' books to be left in their classroom. These books included:

Elkin, B. *Six foolish fishermen*
Armitage, R. *One moonlit night*
Benchley, N. *The several tricks of Edgar Dolphin*
Greenberg, D. *Slugs*
Baker, J. *Home in the sky*
Briggs, R. *Jim and the beanstalk*

Then, because I needed help in choosing books especially for the children, I asked if they could tell me more about themselves as readers by filling out a form — The Heatherington Primary Scale for measuring attitudes to reading. They enjoyed ticking the faces on the sheet to indicate how they felt about various reading activities. I also gave them the interest inventory.

Scale used to assess children's attitudes to reading activities

I explained that each time we met, I would introduce different ways of responding after reading a book, and that I would show them how to try out these ideas. There would also be time to have a chat (a book conference) about a book they had read, with me or the teacher.

Session 2: writing from a different point of view

To help children understand that authors write from different points of view, I devised idea cards to introduce them to this important concept. I began by introducing six varied books, some with ideas for rewriting the story from different points of view outlined on a small card on the front. The books I introduced were

Van Horn, W. *The Big Sneeze*
De Regniers, B. *Red Riding Hood*
Cook, P. *Elmer makes a break*
Harmey, S. *Sharks*
Lavelle, S. *The Big Stink*
Logan, N. *Dinosaur adventure*

My introductions to the books were short, designed to arouse their interest and to provide a guide to the difficulty of the text and the major theme or areas covered by the book. I demonstrated an idea card which asked children to retell the story from another character's point of view. As an example, I rewrote the story of *Little Red Riding Hood* from the wolf's point of view. The copy of my writing was left pinned to a chart headed 'Ideas for getting you off the ground', with a picture of a rocket stuck to it for inspiration.

Then from a list of children ready for a reading-writing conference I chose four children to chat with individually, and the teacher did likewise, while the remainder of the class either read or wrote. In the conferences we discussed the children's view of the book they had read and we responded to their writing and provided suggestions for further reading. Sometimes the children read a small section aloud but I found this took too much of my time and I could gauge more about the children's reading of the book by discussion and by reading their written response.

<u>Red Riding Hood</u> — as told by me, the wolf

Life is hard for a wolf like me. I always seem to be getting into trouble because of my big appetitte. I'm always hungry. Last week I met a friendly little girl in the woods. She was taking food to her Grandmother, but did she offer poor me any? No! I raced off to her Grandmother's house to see if she would share the meal with me when she got there.

After her Grandmother hid in the cupboard because she was so scared of me, I decided to have some fun. I dressed as Grandmother to trick the little girl into giving me the food, but things did not work out that way. The girl screamed out and a rather nasty looking man with an axe scared me away!

So here I am thinking up a new plan to get me some food. I wonder if there are any tasty little pigs around here?

Writing from a different point of view

Session 3: poetry as response to literature

In this session I focused on the idea of writing poetry as a response to a story. I introduced six different books from various genres.

Parr, L.   *Seagull*
Rose, G.   *Scruff*
Klein, R.   *Thingnapped*
Blake, Q.   *The story of the dancing frog*
Kent, J.   *Socks for supper*
Potter, B.   *The complete adventures of Tom Kitten*

I then demonstrated an idea card which suggested that children could write a poem about a book they had read. My attempt at different forms of poetry was inspired by the book *Seagull* and I left the poems on a wall chart for children to refer to later. The teacher and I conferenced with the children after I had modelled this idea.

When I walk along a beach
Seagulls come, just out of reach.
They float on air down to the sand.
It's bread they see in my hand.

SEAGULLS

– after reading
Seagull by L. PARR

The beady eye of a seagull
Looks down from the clear blue sky.
He studies the jetty fishermen
. . . . well- known cry.

Sand
Eat
Angry
Gliding
Underwater
Land
Looks

Seagull
Old seagull
Cross old seagull
Cross old seagull squawks.
He is a bully to the others.

Arched
Back arched
His back arched
His back arched angrily.
He wants the food they have.

[Words about the seagull from the book]

Water
Wings
summer
orange beak
bright eyes
lands precisely
white-feathered body
he swoops and glides
thin, red, lollypop legs
three-toed webbed feet
squeals noisily, beak open,
cleaning and preening
to shelter
sleep at last

An idea card: story editing

Wolf! Wolf! by ROSE

IDEAS
1. This story could have had a sad ending. You write one.

2. Tell what it was that Jason did that was wrong.

Chart of poetry forms used as models

Session 4: making new endings to stories

In this session, I wanted to use books to stimulate the children's thinking about the ways stories are developed with a beginning, middle and end. I discussed an idea card which suggested writing a new ending to a story. I told the story *Wolf! Wolf!* and then with the children's help, I wrote a different ending to the story on the chalk board. I introduced the following books during this session:

Krasilovsky, P. *The man who didn't wash his dishes*
Huddy, Delia *The Tale of the Crooked Crab*
Charlip, R. *What Good Luck, what Bad Luck*
Lavelle, S. *The Disappearing Granny*

Some children then selected books to read and tried out the idea of writing new endings to the stories. This idea was also used by many children in future sessions.

Session 5: vocabulary development

While the other children were reading and writing responses to books, I devoted a whole session to two boys who were having reading difficulties. We looked at *Bobo's Dream* by M. Alexander, a book without a text. The children's inarticulateness made progress difficult, and their lack of recall made writing about the book frustrating. Following a discussion with the teacher we agreed that many of the children needed lots more help with vocabulary to describe books so we decided to tackle this in future sessions.

Session 6: character description

As many of the children commonly used words such as 'nice' and 'good' to describe characters, I devised this session to help build up vocabulary to describe characters. Each child was given the sheet 'A Character' which we compared to the fun sheet done previously to find reading attitudes. The sheet contained vocabulary the children might find useful in both oral description and written description of particular characters.

	A CHARACTER				
	very	somewhat	neither or both	somewhat	very
happy	......	....	....	....	...... unhappy, sad
careful	......	....	....	....	...... clumsy
lucky	......	....	....	....	...... unlucky
clever, smart	......	....	....	....	...... stupid
friendly	......	....	....	....	...... unfriendly
brave	......	....	....	....	...... cowardly, timid
strong	......	....	....	....	...... weak
beautiful	......	....	....	....	...... ugly
gentle	......	....	....	....	...... violent, rough
calm	......	....	....	....	...... excited
proud	......	....	....	....	...... ashamed
good	......	....	....	....	...... bad, horrible
generous	......	....	....	....	...... mean
honest	......	....	....	....	...... dishonest
kind	......	....	....	....	...... unkind, cruel
clean	......	....	....	....	...... dirty
funny	......	....	....	....	...... serious
tidy	......	....	....	....	...... messy
polite	......	....	....	....	...... rude
sensible	......	....	....	....	...... silly
joyful	......	....	....	....	...... miserable

A character sheet

We thought about various well-known characters like the wolf from *Little Red Riding Hood* and worked down the sheet choosing suitable words to describe him.
I then introduced five books:
Klein, R. *The Enemies*
Flack, M. *The story of Ping*
Impey, R. *Who's a clever girl then?*
Porter, W. *Kate Shelley and the midnight express*
Bates, D. *The Belligrumble big foot*

Sandra in "The Enemies"

During a visit to the Museum, Sandra made her mother and Mary-Anna miserable because she behaved so <u>badly</u>.

Before she even left home, Sandra wanted to wear her plastic crash helmet covered in horse pictures, which was <u>rather silly</u>. Her mother said she was a <u>messy</u> dresser, unlike <u>neat</u> Mary-Anna.

On the train Sandra was <u>very</u> unfriendly to Mary-Anna and would not talk to her. As the day continued she became worse because she was so horrible and hard to please. Even the guard told her off for being <u>dirty</u> when she squashed her mouth on a glass display case!

Kate Shelley and the Midnight Express by W. PORTER

IDEA
What can you tell about Kate Shelley?

The Enemies by R. KLEIN

IDEA
Describe one of the girls either when they were enemies or when they were friends

Idea cards: character

The Belligrumble Bigfoot

IDEA
Give a character description of
<u>either</u> Willie Macbeth, the boy
<u>or</u> Willie 'Snorkel' Macbeth
<u>or</u> Williamson Macbeth VC. VC, VC

The Enemies by Robin Klein had an idea card attached to the front suggesting that one of the characters be described. I demonstrated writing a description of one of the main characters, Sandra.

Children were then encouraged to try other idea cards which focused on character description. I found that the children often chose to write character descriptions in later sessions.

Session 7: more about character description

I introduced several more books which had suitable characters to describe.

Tidy, B.   *A day at Cringemound School*
Prokofiev, S.   *Peter and the Wolf*
Dann, M.   *Bernice knows best*
Nicoll, P.   *Meg and Mog*
Viorst, J.   *The tenth good thing about Barney*

At this stage of the program I felt it was particularly valuable for me to move around the working classroom having whispered chats with individuals about what they were doing and offering suggestions about their reading and writing. In that way I could communicate with at least half the class per session. As in all sessions, the teacher conferenced several children while others pursued their own reading and writing activities.

Reading in the library corner

Session 8: reading the literature we created

During this session, I introduced several books I thought the children would enjoy:

Edwards, P.   *Making Damper*
Gretz, Susanna   *Its your turn Roger*
Arkle, P.   *Grandma's own Zoo*
Vaughan, M.   *Wombat Stew*
Stone, B.   *Emergency Mouse*

On this day, however, the children were eager to read the literature that they themselves had created. I had been busily promoting books to them and they thought it was their turn to present their own books to me.

So, besides the usual introductions of new books and suggested ideas, I admired samples of their good work on the walls and chatted with the workers.

Session 9: a consolidation session

This was essentially a catch-up session, so I reminded children to keep their records of books read up-to-date. I had found that following my introductions of new books, many children were ready to drop whatever they were doing and begin a new book. Obviously I was emphasising the books more than the writing! Besides conferencing, I checked records and the children's writing books and I also promoted these books:

Pursell, T. *The Mystery of Lost Beach*
Peet, B. *Jennifer and Josephine*
Kitson, J. *Schools*
Herriot, J. *Moses the kitten*

Session 10: book illustrations

For this session I wanted the children to develop critical skills for forming opinions about picture books. A picture book and a sheet called 'Illustrations' was supplied to each child. I made sure that the picture books showed examples of each technique described on the Illustrations sheet. Using examples found by me and those found by children, we worked our way down the sheet discussing the vocabulary used for describing illustrations and also had a quick look at the list of useful sentence beginnings to use when describing the pictures in books. Some of the picture books we used were:

Pendle, A. *The cat who could fly*
Nikly, M. *The Princess on the mat*
Isenbart, H. *Birth of a duckling*
Grimm, W. *Briar Rose: the Sleeping Beauty*

ILLUSTRATIONS (PICTURES)
Words to help describe them

black & white, pale, faint	.... colorful
dull	.... bright
detailed	.... simple, sketchy, wishy-washy
fine lines	.... bold
warm colors (reds, oranges, yellows)	.... cool colors (blues, greens)
active, busy	.... peaceful, calm
large (fill most of the page)	.... small (only cover a little of the page)
clear, easy to understand	.... vague, hard to follow
text (words) more important	.... pictures more important
almost real like a photograph	.... childlike, strange, hard to work out
painted	.... colored with pencils or crayons
photographs	.... collage (pieces stuck on to make a picture)

SOME USEFUL SENTENCE BEGINNINGS

The illustrations are . . .	Although the text is more important . .
The illustrator has . .	Right from the start . . .
Some of the pictures . . .	Unfortunately . . .
Most pictures . . .	Each animal/character/person . . .
Dull/Bright/Colourful/Large etc. pictures . .	I hardly notice the . . .
Every second page . . .	I was first attracted by the . . .
Throughout the book . . .	I found the . . .

The illustrations sheet

I found this session worked very well, and could have been extended into several sessions as the children enjoyed analysing the different kinds of media used in illustrations.

In conclusion

At the end of the ten-week program the children's attitude towards reading remained very positive and their reading age scores had all increased. Some children still required a lot of teacher guidance in selecting appropriate books and in pursuing writing activities, but most were reading eagerly and beginning to select a combination of the easy-to-read books and books that were more challenging.

Many children went through a stage of reading the easy-to-read books in order to read quickly and compete with others in the class. This had begun to cease as the program became established and as the children realised the program is individual and not competitive.

On reflection, now the program is over I think the essential components in making the program successful were:

- ☐ the continued enthusiasm and co-operation of the classroom teacher;
- ☐ a survey of children's reading interests in order to provide appropriate books;
- ☐ the provision of a bulk loan of books well displayed in the classroom (this loan must be carefully weeded and added to regularly);
- ☐ the setting up of a simple class borrowing system in order to monitor the popularity of books.

I also recommend that if a teacher wants to encourage children to respond to books through writing, the teacher should carefully model examples. The children in the class all chose to respond in a variety of written forms based on what they had observed and tried out in the sessions.

The program also requires a formalised procedure for conferencing in both reading and writing so that all children regularly receive the amount of time they need from an adult. It is essential to have a satisfactory system of recording and keeping track of each child's reading and responses.

In future, if a similar program is conducted in the same school in another classroom, for example, the teachers and I could work towards making a stockpile of successful books with idea cards which could be re-used by other children and other classes.

After this experience I am more and more convinced that the teacher-librarian is a useful resource person who can promote books, reading and writing, to both children and teachers interested in literature-based reading.

Possibly the greatest advantage for children with this program is that once the basic requirements are carried out, for example, the contract, individuals then have the freedom to work at their own pace. The sky is the limit. Boredom need not occur because new materials and ideas are continually being presented.

References

Alexander, J. E. and Filler, R. C. *Attitudes and Reading*. International Reading Association, 1976.

Butler, A. and Turbill, J. *Towards a Reading-Writing Classroom*, PETA, 1984.

Johnson, T. D. and Louis, D. *Literacy through Literature*, Methuen, 1985.

Programs with a special focus

Themes with year 7 classes   7

Deirdre Travers

At Mercedes College all teachers from year 2 to 7 have a literature-based approach to reading. As the teacher-librarian I work closely with the staff in planning and implementing their programs. While some thematic work is done at the year 6 level, at year 7 we introduce a formally structured thematic approach.

The overall aims of the school's literature-based reading program are continued at this level, the primary one being that students enjoy reading. In addition, we want our students to

- [ ] become aware of the range of literature available and so be able to select books that suit their interests and needs;
- [ ] be able to discriminate between the different literary genres;
- [ ] be aware of the aspects of a novel, such as plot, character development, setting and writing styles; and also
- [ ] become discerning in what they read.

At year 7 almost all the children have sufficient reading skills to read widely and independently. At this level we introduce themes to provide a whole-class focus for comparisons and discussion which we hope will further our overall aims for the reading program, as stated above, and also foster in the students deeper insights into themselves, other people and the environment.

The discussions that are encouraged and planned allow the students to

- [ ] extend and enhance their enjoyment of a book;
- [ ] share their emotional responses to literature;
- [ ] clarify their reason for liking or not liking a book or aspects of it; and
- [ ] develop further insights into aspects of life dealt with in a book.

While many of these aims are pursued at other levels in the reading program, at year 7 these aims become a priority and we structure our program more specifically to achieve them. Perhaps the best way to explain our use of themes is to describe the reading program with the 1986 year 7 class.

Theme: country and city life in Australia

At the beginning of the year I met with each of the two year 7 teachers to plan their literature programs. One class was studying rural and urban life in Australia in Social Studies, so the class teacher and I decided to use this theme in the reading program.

We decided on the following three specific goals:

1 Develop a greater understanding of life in the country and the city, both now and in the past.
2 Read examples of a genre that many would not have encountered before, such as biography.
3 Gain knowledge of two Australian authors, namely Colin Thiele and Eleanor Spence.

We agreed that the theme would run for seven weeks and that the students would have a forty-minute discussion period in the library each week. Each student would be asked to read a minimum of four novels in the seven weeks.

I compiled a list of titles that I hoped would offer a wide range of choice for different interests and ability levels. The titles ranged from Christobel Mattingley's

Magpie at Windmill Creek, a very simple, short story for the less able readers in the class, to James Aldridge's *The True Story of Lilly Stubeck*, a complex and sophisticated novel, included to extend the more able readers. The titles were listed with annotations for the students. By having a list of over thirty titles, we hoped to give students a wide choice, but at the same time to encourage a shared experience among children reading the same titles. This sharing is an essential part of the program as it allows meaningful class and group discussion to take place.

The introductory session was held in the library. Each student was given the list and time to read it through. The class teacher and I then explained why the theme was chosen, what we hoped would be the result of reading these titles, and the minimum requirement. Students were then encouraged to talk about the books they had read. I introduced other books that no one in the class had read, giving a brief outline of the story and its setting, and occasionally reading an excerpt. The students then had an opportunity to borrow from the library. As we have multiple copies of many of the titles, most students were able to get their first or second choices. Individual guidance was given to those students who were not able to make an immediate choice and to the two students in the class whose reading ability made guidance necessary.

Booklist for COUNTRY AND CITY LIFE IN AUSTRALIA

Spence, Eleanor   *The October Child*
The story of Douglas, whose life is changed when baby Carl is born. Carl is autistic, and causes the family to move from the country to the city.
The Seventh Pebble
When the Connells move to a small country town, everyone is distrustful because they are Catholics, poor and a large family without a father.
The Year of the Currawong
The Kendalls move from a busy city life, to live in a small country town for a year, and find out all about country towns.
Lillipilly Hill
Harriet and her father love their new home in the Australian countryside, but the rest of the family want to return to England. Set in early Australia.

Thiele, Colin   *The Fire in the Stone*
An adventure story set in an opal mining town in South Australia.
Blue Fin
A story of the tuna fishing industry in South Australia, and boy growing up.
The Sun on the Stubble
The Shadow on the Hills
The Valley Between
Colin Thiele writes about life in the Barossa Valley as he remembers it, with sometimes sad, sometimes funny, and often exciting incidents.
Chadwick's Chimney
Country life near Mount Gambier, and an adventure story.
Albatross Two
Life aboard an oil rig.
The Hammerhead Light
A story set near a lighthouse.

French, Simon	*Cannily, Cannily*
Brinsmead, Hesba	*Longtime Passing*
	Longtime Dreaming
	Once there was a Swagman
Norman, Lilith	*Climb on a Lonely Hill*
Frances, H.	*The Devil Stone*

Two girls living in the Adelaide Hills find strange things happening, after a huge stone rolls down off the hill. When they find a diary from children who had lived there before them, they begin to work out what is happening.

| Ingram, A. B. | *Shudders and Shakes* |

Two collections of short stories, one ghostly, and the other 'tall' tales. Set in the bush.

Mattingley, Christobel	*Magpie at Windmill Creek*
	Duck Bay
	Tiger's Milk
Kenshan, Kerry	*Red and the Heron Street Gang*
Aldridge, J.	*The True Story of Lilly Stubeck*

Set in a country town on the River Murray, this book tells the story of Lilly who belongs to a poor and dishonest family, and her relationship with the richest person in the town.

| Fowler, Thurley | *Wait for me! Wait for me!* |

Set in the Australian riverland, Robert is small and skinny, as well as being accident prone. He longs to be like his three older brothers, big and muscly, and good at school and sport. However he does eventually prove that being small and skinny has its advantages.

	The Green Wind
	Am I Going With You?
Gleeson, Libby	*Eleanor Elizabeth*

Eleanor Elizabeth moves to the country and finds her grandmother's diary, written when she was Elizabeth's age. The diary helps save her from a bushfire.

| Phipson, Joan | *The Cats* |
| | *No Escape* |

Picture Books

Morris, Jill	*The Boy who Painted the Sun*
Mattingley, C.	*The Great Ballagundi Damper Bake*
Walker, K.	*Marty Moves to the Country*
Klein, Robin	*Oodoolay*
Hathorn, E	*The Tram to Bondi Beach*

In the next two weekly library sessions, opportunity was provided for students to discuss the books they had read. If students were having difficulty finding a book they enjoyed, other students were encouraged to give suggestions.

I then introduced the two authors whose books we were going to look at in more detail. In the first week I introduced Colin Thiele and in the second Eleanor Spence. The teacher and I had chosen these authors because the students had read little of their work previously, the settings of the books enhanced our theme and Social Studies topic, both are prolific writers, and we felt their work would appeal to these students. In introducing the authors I gave a brief biography and then introduced their books by briefly outlining the stories and settings, and reading excerpts. I

Groups often discussed topics and reactions to books

read part of the chapter from *Sun on the Stubble* by Colin Thiele where the boys are caught smoking. This had immediate appeal to the students, and Colin Thiele's books immediately became popular. His popularity grew as the unit continued.

Some of the students' comments on Thiele's novels were:

'It (*Fire in the Stone*) was full of adventure and I really liked the reality.'

'*Seashores and Shadows* is the best book I've read; it's funny and action packed.'

'I thought *Coorong Captive* was excellent because I imagine things very clearly and I found this book very true to life because I have been to the Coorong and I know what it is like.'

Eleanor Spence's work did not generate the same enthusiasm, although some of the more confident and mature readers expressed particular enjoyment of *The Seventh Pebble* and *The October Child*.

In the classroom the children had daily silent sustained reading sessions. As well, it was expected that the students would read at home. Many of the more popular titles were borrowed as a classroom loan and kept in the classroom to allow the books to circulate more efficiently, and class waiting lists were established. The class teacher showed videos of *Blue Fin*, *Fire in the Stone* and *Storm Boy* to maintain enthusiasm. The students were given written activities in the classroom which focused on setting and the various aspects of city and country life. Weekly sessions were held in the library in which children talked about books they had read, and encouraged and helped those who were not able to find a book they enjoyed. These discussions were always informal and spontaneous. The children were enthusiastic and supportive of others, asking questions and suggesting books.

A result of this theme was that the students wrote to Colin Thiele, which in turn led to him visiting the school.

As a final activity we invited the other year 7 class who were about to start a similar topic, and the students gave prepared talks on their favorite books. All students were asked to prepare a one-to-two-minute talk to present to the two class groups, in which they said why they liked the book, discussed the setting, and gave an outline of the story.

No formal evaluation, other than the class written work, was attempted. However, the students showed obvious enthusiasm in the weekly class discussions and book introductions, and although it is impossible to judge with any certainty, we felt the Social Studies program was enhanced.

Theme: Man and his Environment

The other year 7 class began with the theme 'War and Relationships'. We hoped to explore the effect of war upon people, and show how friendship and love can survive this. We did not have a written list, books were simply introduced to the class by the classroom teacher, the principal and myself. Despite the enthusiasm of the three adults for the topic, the children showed few signs of enthusiasm for the books, and expressed some relief when the topic was finished. It would appear that in contrast to the theme of the other year 7 class, the students had neither the experience nor the maturity required for this topic.

When we then introduced the theme 'Man and his Environment', once again a Social Studies theme, and included on this list many of the books by Australian authors, particularly Colin Thiele, the children were enthusiastic in their responses and read widely.

The choice of theme is particularly important, and from my experience I believe the theme needs to be within the range of the students' experiences to work successfully at the beginning of year 7. Later in the year, when the experiences and maturity of the students had increased, we were able to introduce books outside their range of experiences. In the third term, we began the theme 'International Relations' including many of the titles which were rejected in Term 1. These were read and enjoyed.

Themes: Against the Odds; Myself and Others

In term two both year 7 teachers expressed the desire to expand the experiences of the students, and to try to extend their understanding of people from other backgrounds and develop a sympathy for the needs of others. This arose from an uncaring attitude shown by some of the students towards others. With one class we used the theme 'Against the Odds' and the book list included titles which showed children in difficult and survival situations, in which the children not only overcome the odds, but also grow through this experience.

In the other class we used the theme 'Myself and Others' and this included books set in Australia, in the United States, England and other countries. This complemented the Social Studies theme, 'The needs of young Australians'. Although both teachers and I would have liked to use the one theme, 'Against the Odds', we would not have had sufficient books. It is essential when using themes to have all the listed books available, and multiple copies of the popular titles. We have class loans of the very popular titles, and I try to collect many of the titles on the list, and have these available for borrowing during library visits.

We used a similar approach to the one previously described. However, in order to have a shared experience we required that the class doing 'Against the Odds' read one of four books. These were *Goodnight Mister Tom*, *The Cay*, *The boy who was afraid*, and *Dear Mr Henshaw*. As in Term 1, regular weekly discussions were held in the library, with both the teacher and me leading the discussions.

Because we had the specific aims of increasing the students' awareness and sympathy for others, we decided discussion groups which focused on these issues were the best approach. With 'Against the Odds', we arranged the class in three groups so that all the children in the group had read the same book. The Junior School Co-ordinator took one group to discuss *Goodnight Mister Tom*, the class teacher took a group to discuss *Dear Mr Henshaw* and I took a group to discuss *The Cay*. We agreed to discuss the following points:

- ☐ How did the character(s) survive?
- ☐ Could you have survived the way they did?
- ☐ Did the book character have any choices?
- ☐ What choices would you have made?
- ☐ How did the character change in the story?
- ☐ How does the book compare to others you read on this theme?

These discussion groups were very successful. All the students were eager to participate, and made many perceptive and sympathetic comments about the situations in the book. When discussing *The Cay*, students talked about 'courage and will to survive'. One student said he 'didn't think he would have saved Phillip if he had been shipwrecked' and another said he 'would have wanted to die but would have lived to make up for Timothy dying'. All of the students seemed able to empathise with the book characters and to imagine themselves in these situations. The two other teachers reported equal success with their groups. When discussing *Goodnight Mister Tom*, a child said that his classmates, after reading of the death of Zach, no longer avoided mentioning the death of his father.

Discussion groups were also held with the other class. While the students showed an understanding of and a sympathy to the needs of others, because the groups lacked the common experience of one book the groups did not have the unity or quality of discussion of the first class. We will in future try to ensure that children have a common experience by reading one of a specified small number of books as we did with 'Against the Odds'.

Recording the group's ideas

Booklist for AGAINST THE ODDS

Arundel, H.	*The high house*
Baillie, A.	*Little brother*
Bawden, Nina	*Carrie's war*
	The peppermint pig
Burnford,	*The incredible journey*
Carr, Roger V.	*Firestorm*
Cleary, Beverly	*Dear Mr Henshaw*
Dejong, Meindert.	*The house of Sixty Fathers*
French, S.	*Cannily, cannily*
Godden, Rumer	*The diddakoi*
George, Jean	*My side of the mountain*
Hautzig, E.	*The Endless Steppe*
Holm, Anne	*I am David*
Kerr, J.	*When Hitler stole pink rabbit*
Kelleher, Victor	*Papio*
	Master of the Grove
Klein, Robin	*Boss of the pool*
	People might hear you
	Hating Alison Ashley
Magorian, Michelle	*Goodnight Mister Tom*
Mattingley, C.	*New patches for old*
Montgomery, L. M.	*Anne of Green Gables*
Morris, Judy K.	*The crazies and Sam*
Moskin, J.	*I am Rosemarie*
Norman, L.	*Climb a lonely hill*
O'Brien, Robert	*Mrs Frisby and the rats of NIMH*
	Z for Zachariah
O'Dell, Scott	*Island of the Blue Dolphins*
Patterson, K.	*The bridge to Terabithia*
	The great Gilly Hopkins
Porter, Eleanor H.	*Pollyanna*
Roy, Thomas	*The curse of the turtle*
Reiss, J.	*The upstairs room*
Southall, Ivan	*Finn's folly*
	Ash Road
Spence, Eleanor	*The October child*
	The leftovers
Shyer, Marlene F.	*Welcome home Jellybean*
Sherrey, S.	*A pair of Jesus boots*
Serraillier, I.	*The silver sword*
Sperry, Armstrong	*The boy who was afraid*
Turner, E.	*Seven little Australians*
Thiele, Colin	*Fire in the stone*
	February dragon
Taylor, T.	*The Cay*
Voigt, Cynthia	*Homecoming*
	Dicey's song
Wilder, L.	*Little house in the big woods*

Other themes

In previous years we have used several other themes successfully. 'Growth and development', in which we read books which explore the physical and emotional growth of young people, has been very successful when read in conjunction with this health topic in Term 3. In this we require all students to read two books by Judy Blume, *Are you there God, It's me Margaret* and *Then again maybe I won't*. These books focus on the physical and emotional development of girls (*Are you there God*) and boys (*Then again maybe I won't*). In the group discussion of these books, all sniggering and giggling that was previously apparent when these topics were mentioned is gone. The students discuss the growth and development of the boys and girls openly and honestly, when all have the same experience of the book.

'Protecting People's Rights and Property' was another theme read in conjunction with this Social Studies topic.

Reporting back to the whole class

Conclusion

This year, as in previous years, we have evaluated the success of the thematic use of literature, by asking the students how they felt about reading and using themes. Most said they enjoyed using the themes although 'not all the time'. Many said they had read and enjoyed books they would not otherwise have read. Many said they liked to have the guidance, and without it 'I don't know what to read'. They agreed that although the books were on the same theme 'they don't all seem the same'. These responses were similar to those of previous years. Because of these responses we will continue to ensure that the students have choice within the theme, and to allow alternate periods of total free choice with those of thematic reading. We will continue using the program because it is enjoyed by both students and teachers, it widens the reading and experiences of the students, and enhances the classroom learning program.

Programs with a special focus

A Big Book and poetry emphasis   8

Maria Woodhouse

Children acquire literacy in much the same way that they learn to speak. They learn because they want to participate, make sense of the language around them and are not afraid to take risks. If they have seen people around them making use of print, children will expect to use print in similar ways and will imitate the reading behavior they see. Another important influence in their reading is the background knowledge that they bring to any text; the more relevant information they already have about a text, the easier will it be to read. My reading program with a composite year 3/4 class is based on these beliefs about learning to read. The ideas have formed mainly from my own observations of how children respond best to reading and also from my reading in this area.

Poetry has pride of place in my literature-based reading program for several reasons. First, I believe that poetry is the best language that is available and therefore children should engage with it. Second, poetry can excite a positive response to written language and therefore facilitate reading and writing. Third, poetry is a sadly neglected area of literature.

Before telling how I introduced poetry in my classroom I will describe the essentials of my reading program: time to listen to stories and time to read. These are crucial to my program because of my conviction that children learn to read by reading and that what children bring to print influences the meaning they will gain from it. I will also discuss the role of Big Books in providing reading experiences, particularly for the less confident readers.

Listening to stories

Through listening to stories told and read the children develop knowledge of how stories work, they build up the store of words that they understand and also refine their appreciation of what stories and books have to offer. In my class the children hear stories read aloud at least twice a day, I tell them stories and they listen to taped stories.

Every day I have two sessions for reading aloud to the class: a ten-minute session in the morning, and a five- to ten-minute session during reading time. As well, whenever we find we have five minutes to spare during the day, usually when we have packed up and are waiting for one of the many sirens, I take the opportunity to read some more. I look forward to these sessions, especially when the children are enjoying the story every bit as much as I am. We lose ourselves together in a shared experience of fantasy, adventure, humor, or whatever emotion is elicited by the story.

I like to have a serialised novel in progress, where the children just listen. But I regularly use what we call a 'class novel', of which I have several copies so that children who want to can be reading it for themselves. The less able readers, in particular, clamor to follow a story in their own book. The following are some novels successfully used for reading aloud.

Milne, A. A.   *Winnie the Pooh*
              House at Pooh Corner
White, E. B.   *Charlotte's Web*
Lewis, C. S.   *The Lion, The Witch and the Wardrobe, The Magician's Nephew*

Blume, J.   *Tales of a Fourth Grade Nothing*
Robinson, B. *The Worst Kids in the World*
Kastner, E.   *Emil and the Detectives*

In addition to the books I read aloud, once a week the children can choose to listen to taped stories such as *Paddington* and *Olga da Polga* on the listening post in the class. There are many tapes like these available (from KGC Records and Tapes, St Peters, NSW, for example). In this period other children have the opportunity to read aloud plays that I have available in the class. The children in my class love to perform, so when some of them have sufficiently rehearsed a play they are invited to present it to the rest of the class. Needless to say, these plays are a popular activity.

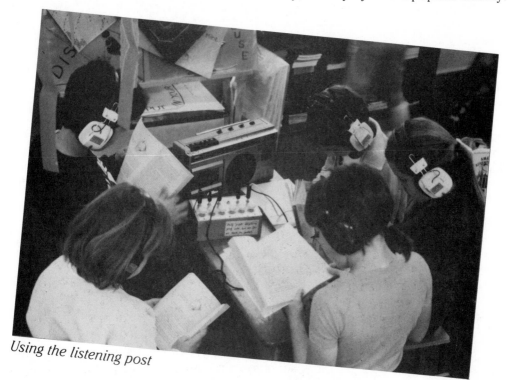

Using the listening post

While I have long accepted reading aloud as integral to my reading program, it is only recently that I have told stories rather than read them to my class. I was intrigued by storytellers and their art, I realised that the constant eye contact available to a storyteller commands attention and ensnares imagination, and was eventually challenged to hold the children in the spell of a story myself. In the words of Mem Fox (1980),

> You never lose contact with your audience, and, more importantly, they never lose contact with you. In reading you cut off the audience contact and re-establish it, and cut it off and re-establish it ad infinitum. Not the most brilliant story reader in the world could succeed with the success of a brilliant storyteller.

When I first took up the challenge to tell stories rather than read them, I set myself the task of learning one story a week to tell the class. At first I found it nerve-racking. The mere thought of telling a story from memory made my mind numb with fright. But I persisted and began by reciting the very familiar and repetitious 'I Know an Old Lady'. As a starter this bolstered my courage and I stayed with familiar stories for a while.

The encouragement I received from the class, their attentiveness and the confidence I gained with these well-known stories, helped me to discipline myself to telling at least one story a week.

I am still not confident about telling long stories, so I tend to stick with short repetitious ones that take only a few minutes. Aesop's fables are very good to begin with as they are short and easy to learn. Traditional tales are also popular and relatively easy to learn because of their predictability. My main sources for these stories were:

Haviland, V.	*The Fairy Tale Treasury*, Puffin, 1974
Grimm	*Grimm's Household Stories*, Macmillan, 1979
Traditional	*Fifty Famous Fairytales*, Whitman, 1979

Time to read

It is only by reading that the skills of reading can be mastered, so a daily time to read a chosen book silently is essential in my program. We have a set routine everyday for this. Ten to fifteen minutes are allotted immediately after lunch. The children walk straight into the classroom, quickly take up their books, and settle themselves comfortably around the classroom to read in undisturbed silence. Our reading corner is furnished with a few bean bags and cushions and the children share these companionably, stretch out on the carpet or sit at their desks while I read a book at my desk. The rules are simple and soon learnt and the children follow the routine easily.

☐ Only reading is allowed.
☐ Children must have enough reading material for the whole session.
☐ Talking is banned.
☐ No movement around the room is allowed.

Big Books

Big Books are a regular part of the reading program. They are not only another way for children to experience good literature, but in providing a shared reading experience, they enable the less able readers to gain confidence and skills for reading. I use this approach with these readers regularly, and generally involve the whole class when introducing a new Big Book. All the children love the Big Books, so the 'Big Book Group' (the less able readers) does not feel disadvantaged by the special work that they do with me.

Big Books used in the Program (all Ashton Scholastic):

Blackburn, C.	*Grant the Ant*
	The Thing from Somewhere
Bonne-Rose	*I Know an Old Lady*
Chance, E.	*Just in Time for the King's Birthday*
Gale, J.	*Neat and Scruffy*
Gelman, R.	*More Spaghetti I Say!*
Traditional	*The Gingerbread Man*
Handy, L.	*Boss for a Week*
Ivemey, J.	*Adventures of the Three Blind Mice*
Traditional	*The Three Billy Goats Gruff*
Littledale, F.	*The Magic Fish*
Lock, S.	*Hubert Hunts his Hum*
Mayer, M.	*What do you do with a Kangaroo?*
Reece, J.	*Lester and Clyde*
Rose, G.	*Trouble in the Ark*

Silent reading

The reading corner

Readalong Rhythms

Baxter, J.	*Rain*
Traditional	*Chinny-chick, Fiddle-i-fee*
Halloran, M.	*The Great Invention*
	The Scientist
Hucklesby, H.	*It Came to Tea*
	Joe Giant
Traditional	*I Know an Old Lady*
Prujean, D.	*At the Movies*
Randell, B.	*The Hen and Sly Fox*
	Ten Big Dinosaurs
	Ten Little Boats
Readhead, J.	*The Strange Loud Noise*
	The Itchy Witch
	The Brontosaurus

I use all the Big Books listed here as well as Big Books we make in class. They are so popular that it is difficult at times to keep up with the children's demand for more. Many of the books are in rhyme, which the children like, and helps their predictions. Because the children love these books and there is so much support in the text and from the readers sitting around them, they have little difficulty in reading them. Even the more difficult text of some of the books does not deter the children from reading them over and over again. And the more practice they get the easier it is for them to read.

I use the Big Books to help the struggling readers to develop strategies for getting meaning from the print without relying too much on phonics. I demonstrate how the different cues help the reader make sense, I suggest strategies for anticipating phrases and words, we talk about ways we 'work out' words that don't come easily, we predict covered words and check our predictions, we discuss how we know what will be on the next page. The stories with rhyme, rhythm and refrains add to the enjoyment of the shared reading and make predictions easy.

Cloze procedure is often part of our Big Book activity and we use the sliding apparatus provided with the Ashton books to cover selected words. My deletions are at first highly predictable for the reader, to ensure success.

Poetry

Poetry is not 'taught' in my class, rather it is shared and enjoyed. My aim is to develop a delight and love for poetry which will in turn urge the children to seek out their own poems to enjoy and share with others.

I read a poem to the class every day. Whenever possible children are encouraged to join in on a familiar line or a refrain, and they do this spontaneously. Each day I also invite children to share their favorites with the class.

The children's response in my year 3/4 class was interesting. Each morning for a week I began our reading sessions with a poem and invited the children to contribute poems as well. Only three children responded for the entire first week. Every day for this week the same three children stood up and read their favorite poems to the class. These are the poems I shared:

Dennis, C. J.	Hist!
	The Triantiwontigongolope
	(*A Book for Kids*, Angus & Robertson, 1976)
Silverstein, Shel	Barry
	Hammock
	Overdues
	Something Missing
	(*A Light in the Attic*, Cape, 1985)
Milne, A. A.	Bad Sir Brian Botany
	The Christening
	Disobedience
	(*When we were Very Young*, Methuen, 1972)
Riev, E. V.	Sir Smasham Uppe
	(*Moths and Moonshine*, Rigby, 1977)
Farjeon, E.	Cats
	(*First Poetry Book*, Oxford, 1979)

The second week brought a radical change. Every day when I asked for children to share poems, more and more volunteered, so that by Friday nearly every child had read a favorite poem to the class. What better practice could they have of reading aloud!

The other astounding thing that happened was that during silent reading time children would sit and avidly devour poetry books with the result that at the end of

Home-made Big Books

Poet-tree

Poetry book display

these daily sessions I had children clamoring to share with the rest of the class poems they had found. As this entailed only five or ten minutes, I agreed, and once again was surprised to see how many of the 'reluctant' readers wanted to share in this way.

By the end of the third week some children were organising themselves into small groups for choral reading and others were learning poetry by heart to recite to the class. Even the children with reading difficulties joined in these activities. Since many of the Big Books being used in the class were poems, these children found they had ample material of their own to present to the class. My class loves performing, and poetry provided them with an exciting new medium for their dramatic talents.

It was a short step from here to writing their own poems. The children were eager to do this and their original compositions were displayed on our poet-tree along with favorite poems that children have copied out.

Poetry had 'caught on' in the class. The children were now hearing, appreciating, selecting, reading, performing and writing poems. I made sure there were plenty of poetry books available in the class and had a whole pin-up board and display shelves given over to poetry. Some children showed initiative in searching out poetry books from home and libraries to share with the class. Even readers whom I had regarded as reluctant were joining the list of children waiting to share a poem.

Some of our favorite poetry books

Agar, K.	*Nothing Serious*, Evans, 1973
Allen, J.	*A Bad Case of Animal Nonsense*, Godine
Brand, J.	*Moths and Moonshine*, Rigby, 1977
Butler, D.	*For Me Me Me*, Hodder and Stoughton, 1983
Cole, W.	*Beastly Girls and Ghastly Boys*, Methuen, 1975
	Oh that's Ridiculous, Methuen, 1972
Danby, M.	*The 2nd Armada Book of Limericks*, Armada, 1978
Dennis, C. J.	*Book for Kids*, Angus & Robertson, 1976
Dugan, M.	*The Moving Skull*, Hodder and Stoughton, 1981
	The Puffin Fun Book, Puffin, 1980
	Stuff and Nonsense, Collins, 1974
Eliot, T. S.	*Old Possum's Book of Practical Cats*, Faber, 1971
Factor, J.	*Far Out Brussel Sprout*, Oxford, 1984
Fatchen, M.	*Songs for my Dog and other People*, Kestrel, 1980
Foster, J.	*A First Poetry Book*, Oxford, 1979
	A Second Poetry Book, Oxford, 1980
	A Fourth Poetry Book, Oxford, 1982
Giles, B.	*Second Australian Poetry Book*, Oxford, 1983
Hoffmann, H.	*Struwwelpeter*, Blackie, 1978
Hughes, T.	*Meet My Folks*, Puffin, 1977
Ireson, B.	*The Beaver Book of Funny Rhymes*, Beaver Books/Hamlyn, 1980
Jackson, H.	*The Complete Nonsense of Edward Lear*, Faber, 1969
Milligan, S.	*A Book of Milligrams*, Puffin, 1975
Milne, A. A.	*The Christopher Robin Verse Book*, Methuen, 1974
	The Hums of Pooh, Methuen, 1984
	Now we are Six, Methuen, 1972
	When we were Young, Methuen, 1972
Paterson, A. B.	*Bush Christening*, Collins, 1976
	Geebung Polo Club, Dorr-McLeod, 1984
	Man from Ironbark, Collins, 1974
	Mulga Bill's Bicycle, Collins, 1973
	Waltzing Matilda, Collins, 1973
Petrie, R.	*Lion Book of Humorous Verse*, Lion, 1973
Reeves, J.	*The Merry Go Rounds*, Puffin, 1971
Seuss, Dr	*Fox in Socks*, Collins, 1966
	Green Eggs and Ham, Collins, 1962
	Horton Hears a Who, Collins, 1976
	How the Grinch Stole Christmas, Collins, 1973
	The Lorax, Collins, 1972
	One Fish Two Fish Red Fish Blue Fish, Collins, 1960
	The Sneeches, Collins, 1965
	Thidwick the Big Hearted Moose, Collins, 1968
	Yertle the Turtle, Collins, 1963

Silverstein, S.   *A Light in the Attic*, Cape, 1985
                   Where the Sidewalk Ends, Cape, 1984
Stevenson, R.L. *A Child's Garden of Verse*, Airmont, 1969
Untermeyer, L.   *Golden Treasury of Poetry*, Golden Press, 1974

Other aspects of my reading program

There are, of course, other aspects of my reading program that are essential to its working smoothly and successfully. The main ones are:

☐ an individualised reading program that allows for children to select their own books, and to read, listen and respond every day to written language;

☐ regular individual conferences in which each child has the opportunity to talk about what he or she has been reading, while I can check on how each child's reading is progressing; and

☐ recording procedures in the form of a 'conference log' where I record the children's understanding of their books, their reading strategies, their attitudes and their preferences. Complementing the teacher's log is each child's 'reading log' in which the children record details of the book being read, dates of beginning and finishing it, and comments. I have found the 'book report sheets' from *Into Books* (1984) useful in providing interesting and varied formats for the children to record this information.

Poetry will always be a regular aspect of my reading program. Not only does poetry provide a way for my class to regularly enjoy enriching experiences together, but it plays a significant part in the children's development as independent, enthusiastic readers.

Reference _____

Thomas, R. and Perry, A. *Into Books: 101 Literature Activities for the Classroom*, Oxford University Press, 1984.

Fox, Mem *Thereby Hangs a Tale*, South Australian College of Advanced Education, Adelaide, 1980.

Programs with a special focus

Preparing for high school 9

Andrew Phillips

Over the last eight years of teaching secondary English, most of them in a country Area School, I have seen many students become non-readers. The main reason that has always been given is 'not enough time'. This is understandable when one considers that the time allocated to reading in secondary schools may be one period a week for private reading. In some programs no time at all is allocated. Students are expected to find time at home for reading for pleasure. However, there often seem to be too many other attractions and too little time to do them, to waste time sitting down with a book.

Since reading in the primary school can be allocated as many as eight periods a week, it seems the ideal time for children to be turned onto reading and to find time in school for plenty of it. With the co-operation of the class teacher in a year 7 class at Lock Area School in South Australia, I trialled a literature-based reading program aimed at developing in the students a more positive attitude to reading, in preparation for secondary school. I worked with the class over a thirteen-week term.

The class was chosen for a number of reasons:

☐ The year 7 level was chosen because I wanted these students to be aware of and familiar with a variety of stories and novels before they entered secondary school, where greater demands are made upon students' time, in school and at home.

☐ The students of the class had shown that they were not interested in reading the texts of the basal reading schemes, even though the class had access to the six most popular schemes. A survey conducted at the beginning of the year showed that a majority of the class disliked the incompleteness of many of the stories, they said that they had to read the whole of each reader before progressing to the next, and they were tired of the group reading approach.

☐ It was a small class of seventeen students and, within my own time-table, more accessible to me than other classes in the school.

There were three main aims that I wanted to achieve:

☐ to introduce the students to a variety of books on a range of themes;
☐ to encourage students to be selective in their choice of reading;
☐ to encourage the students to expand their responses to reading.

To achieve these aims I planned to have available a wide selection of books, regular time in class to read, frequent reading aloud to the students and a system for keeping track of the students' reading. In addition I wanted to find reading material that would appeal to reluctant readers.

A wide variety of books was essential to the program, so a bulk loan of fifty books was made from the library. I involved several of the children in this selection by having them decide with me the books to be borrowed, and also by encouraging them to select titles that interested them from up-to-date publishers' pamphlets and catalogues. If their selections were not already in the catalogue then a list was kept for possible future purchase.

The chosen books were piled onto a large table in the class's reading area to ensure that the children handled many books in their search for one to read. The covers, not merely the spines, were visible and the pile more enticing than a neat stack.

Time for reading was found by programming a daily period of Uninterrupted

Silent Sustained Reading, when I read as well as the children. At first these sessions lasted about fifteen minutes but increased through the term until they were usually thirty-five minutes long. In addition to USSR, time was set aside each week for talking about books and for reading aloud favorite parts of the books being read.

Another important regular part of the program was reading aloud. Twice a week I read aloud from a class novel. In addition, students selected parts of their books to read aloud to the rest of the class. Initially, the less confident readers were reticent in reading to the class, but gradually as more and more of the group took a turn, the others gained confidence and found parts they wanted to share as well. The more competent readers generally searched out an extract to read aloud from each book they read — generally from a different book each week. Over the term the most obvious sign of the class's changing attitude to reading was their increasing willingness and enthusiasm to share what they were reading with the rest of the students.

The students filled in individual record cards so that they and I could keep track of what they had read. As well, in each book in the class collection there was a card like the ones used for library borrowing which showed who was currently reading the book. It also allowed students to check who else had read that book so that past readers' opinions of the book could be sought before reading it or afterwards.

Introducing a variety of literature

I used Australian short stories, historical novels and fiction, science fiction and biographies to awaken interest in stories and books that the students might otherwise not have read. I began with Australian short stories. These proved popular with the group. I selected the stories for reading aloud from the following:

Lawson, Henry	*Henry Lawson's Best Stories* selected by Cecil Mann, Angus & Robertson, 1967
Brissenden, R. F. (ed.)	*Southern Harvest*, Macmillan, 1967
Williams-Ellis, A. and	*Out of this World*, Blackie, 1960
Owen, M. Thiele,	*Australian Short Stories*, Rigby, 1963
Colin (ed.)	*Novels and Short Stories for Secondary English*, Education Department of South Australia

Stories that raised a lot of discussion were 'The Golden Shanty' by Edward Dyson, 'The Batting Wizard from the City' and 'The Foal', both by Dal Stivens, and 'The Loaded Dog' by Henry Lawson. These stories contained humorous incidents that the students readily related to.

History, when associated with a book, seems to immediately put students off reading. This is possibly because some authors of historical fiction presume some historical background knowledge of their readers. To introduce historical fiction, I read *The Silver Sword*, by Ian Serraillier. The characters and situations are believable and convincing, and the children had some background knowledge through seeing films and television programs set around the Second World War. The story allows many openings for discussion on topics such as 'Is it right to steal if you are hungry?' and 'Were the enemy soldiers bad, and all Allied soldiers good?'

This story was followed by a collection of local histories and by having local historians talk to the students about how they collected material for their books. These local histories, such as Laurel Spriggs' *Cleve on the Yednarie Plain* and *Across the Bar at Waterloo Bay* by the Elliston Centenary Committee, had been published in the previous few years. There are also available in our area many written histories of local families which have interesting material in them. These are particularly appealing as the students enjoy tracing lineage and anecdotes about people not far removed from themselves.

I felt that this approach was important not only because it gave the students information and an interest in their local area, but because they could realise that history has not stopped. History is about real people, places and events and they themselves are part of history.

As a follow-up to this history focus, the students were asked to read one historical fiction book themselves. This was well received as the students now saw history and historical fiction in a new light. I found my broad knowledge of authors and their work valuable in helping the students find books that catered for the range of capabilities and interests.

Science fiction may well be the most difficult area of literature to introduce to young readers. Like adults, children are either SciFi fans and read it avidly, or leave it alone completely. I chose to introduce science fiction with the help of avid readers and collectors of that genre from the community. The introduction to the books and explanations of them for the students came not from me but from a farmer and a bank clerk who were able to talk about their enthusiasm for these books and also of their particular preferences within this genre.

I then read the students the story, *The Ruum*, by Arthur Porges (Blackie, 1960). They appreciated the story with its particular twist at the end, and had some original ideas to put forward on how to escape the Ruum. I was not able to create a rush for science fiction, but some students did make an effort to appreciate this type of book, and all now have a better understanding of what science fiction can offer them.

To introduce biographies to the class, I invited several citizens who had a tale to tell about early days in the district to come and talk about their early lives. Elderly citizens are great for spinning yarns about their old school days, and life without modern amenities and entertainment. The retired teacher of the original town school, some of the first students of a nearby historic Siding School, and of the now defunct one-teacher schools were able to make the past come alive with their stories, and I linked these anecdotes and experiences with sections of *Saddle in the Kitchen* by Enga Smith and *Mad as Rabbits* by Elizabeth Lane. These books interested many students in reading the other biographies that were then made available to them.

Travelogues seemed a logical extension from the previous genres, but there was not time to introduce these to the students within the term. I had planned to use local people who had travelled around Australia and other countries to tell about their experiences. Many of our students have never left the Eyre Peninsula, so this type of literature is important in offering a broader understanding of other places and people.

Teaching the art of selection

There appears to be little research done on training children in choosing what to read. In developing this art of selection I am not referring to the art of promotion or motivation, but of becoming a discriminating reader, of being able to discern what a book has to offer a particular reader — behind the glossy cover, the blurb on the back, the title and a skimming of the first few pages. Plots, settings and characters are not immediately evident in books, unlike the visual media. It takes a keen reader or a mature one to persevere with some really worthwhile books.

To develop this art, and at the same time overcome the problem of 'There's nothing to read!' or 'What can I read?', I have asked students to take an active part in the school's book buying. This has proved to be highly motivational in allowing individuals to follow particular interests, whether they be hobbies, sport or fiction.

Co-operation between the teacher-librarian, the rest of the teaching staff and the students is basic in developing a selection of books that interests all those who are to use it. Children should be involved right from the beginning in the book purchasing process of a school. With this sort of co-operation, a book collection can then be seen as a selection 'we have made', rather than books 'for you to read'. At our school this co-operation is achieved in the following ways:

□ through having a teacher-librarian who is genuinely interested in student and staff interests and who makes an effort to discover their reactions to books and their current needs;

□ through involving the teacher-librarian in developing the school's curriculum and the class program;

□ through giving students access to publishers' catalogues, accepting their suggestions and recommendations and acting on them in time for the students to see the results of their recommendations.

Displays of book advertisements, catalogues and brochures that are constantly being sent to the school are used to promote books and assist book discussions and selection. Books that the students select can contribute to the library, to the class or to students' own private collections. The reluctant reader occasionally suggests material that appeals to him or her.

Most books can be ordered on approval and returned if they do not come up to expectations, or are not suitable. Before ordering any, the student has to check that the book is not already in the library and when the book arrives, it is first read by the orderer, sometimes even before it has been processed for the library. By using this approach, the children are learning to develop selection tools — the publishers' blurb or summary of the book and a first reading. After experience of this process, some students become very critical of the advertising, as what is stated on the publishers' materials is not always a true indication of the book. This provokes important discussion and awareness of advertising intentions and techniques that is relevant to other products. Film advertising is often referred to as another example, and alternative and more reliable means of finding out about books and films are discussed.

Many country children are unable to peruse material in bookshops, because there are none in their locality. Therefore, when a visiting bookseller and publishers' representative display their wares at the school, it is done in the library, and the children throughout the school are encouraged to look at the material and recommend selection or suggest titles. Once this is done, then the procedure for ordering and previewing is followed.

In fact, children are the best promoters of books to their peers. Given the opportunity, they will talk about the books they are reading with as much enthusiasm and excitement as they talk about last night's horror movie or a television serial. The teacher can encourage this sort of sharing by providing regular times for book talk, showing genuine interest through questioning, comparing and reading a student's recommendation, and by inviting and encouraging students to question and comment on each others' views.

As well as all these promotion, display and encouraging strategies, the teacher also must check that each child can use the various parts of a book that are helpful in making an informed selection. Occasionally these skills need to be revised or taught with the whole class, a small group, or with one child. Generally, the teacher does not need to do this; other members of the class can, when invited, show the ways *they* find books they enjoy.

Responding to literature

Having children review, summarise or retell a story can often discourage reading rather than support it. If students perceive the purpose of reading a novel to be one of these exercises, there is little room for the joy and satisfactions of reading just for the sake of becoming involved in another world, another time and ways of behaving. Claire Woods writes, 'Response to literature contains at least three elements — sustained contact with a book, ownership of the process of taking meaning from text, and sharing the experience and reactions to literature' (*Contact*, 1982). It is with these three elements in mind that I encourage students to respond in ways of their own choice. Not all children choose to formally respond; sometimes the experience with the novel can be too personal, too close to home and too confusing to share. The need for privacy needs to be respected by the teacher. And sometimes the child is enthused to immediately find and read another book. Reading another book may well be the best form of response.

These are some suggestions I made for students to extend their response to reading:

☐ Create a cartoon comic strip (8 to 12 frames) with captions to convey the main idea of a chapter or incident in the story. This calls on the creative and interpretive skills of the reader in isolating an incident and maintaining continuity within a limited medium.

☐ Write a short play of a selection from the story, to be enacted by a small group. The effort put into the writing must be valued and made worthwhile by an opportunity for a final production before an audience, whether it is of classmates, other classes or parents.

☐ Poetry writing is another option, that children approach reluctantly at first. But once they have achieved some satisfaction with the final result, they become more willing to respond in this way. Again, having an audience to appreciate the poetry is a strong motivation. Giving the students model forms to work from gives them confidence to begin and eventually to experiment with different forms. Here is one student's piece about 'the Fiddler', a swagman in Alan Marshall's *I Can Jump Puddles*.

The Fiddler
He wandered around
Camping under the trees
Having nowhere to go
To sleep or to feed.
Old and dirty he shuffles along
Passing over the same track.
A shadow,
Slowly moving among the trees.

He lay down silently,
His old friend, Fire, beside him,
Drinking from the bottle
Nearly at its end.
A great teller of tales
The fiddler used to be, but
Now he sleeps soundly
Beneath the friendly trees.

☐ Students keep a reading diary where they jot down connections, comments or questions that they have as they read, or write a diary of one of the characters in the story. The character diary helps a reader to see the point of view of one of the characters and to better understand that character's relationships with the other people in the book. It also helps understanding of the time and sequence of the novel. Some writers, such as Ivan Southall, use an episodic style and the story jumps from one setting to the next. A diary of one of the characters helps to maintain the flow of the story.

☐ Share the story by talking about it or a part of it. Once the students have begun to appreciate hearing or hearing about interesting, dramatic or humorous sections, they enjoy doing the same themselves. I put time aside for these discussions; the teller must have an audience.

☐ Write as a response. Such writing should not be seen as an imposed task, but as an extension of the pleasure of reading. For this reason I encourage the students to discover ways that best suit their reactions to a book. I make several options available:

> Extend the story one more chapter. What happened next?
> Change the ending.
> Make the villain win.
> Write a newspaper report of the story.
> Compare the story or character with another.
> Change the time or setting of the story.
> Change the sex or age of the leading character.
> Relate the story to your own experiences.

These options become more accessible after we have tried each as a class, with me as an active participator. The students then have a better idea of what each piece of writing involves.

☐ Art and craft are ways of responding without the demands of the written word or having to speak to an audience. This form can, however, increase a student's understanding of the story as do the other forms of response. Illustrations for a story, of a character or the most exciting part all require the student to recall, select and decide what will be depicted.

☐ Develop a project of a personal interest. This was a spontaneous development for one student who, after reading Colin Thiele's *Storm Boy*, produced an excellent wall chart on birds of the Coorong. This particular interest demanded much careful researching and preparation.

This list of activities is by no means exhaustive, but represents the main activities undertaken by the students. Time is provided as part of the class reading time for these responses to be developed. Students also often elect to work on their responses in free-choice time and at home.

The reluctant reader

No matter what approach to reading a teacher uses, there will still be some students who are not keen to read — the students who can read but choose not to. Their stock answer is 'There's nothing to read'. This usually means that they have not found pleasure in their previous reading experiences and they don't have the necessary skills for searching out suitable materials for themselves.

In looking for reading materials to motivate these students I have found the following series successful:

☐ The *Asterix* series by Goscinny and Uderzo (Hodder and Stoughton) suits students who have trouble concentrating on pages of print. They will often settle down with these books, published in cartoon form, for a whole lesson. Not only that, they will return again and again to reread them and find more. The students may not fully grasp the puns or the references to historical events, but they do learn that they can enjoy reading and be successful at it.

☐ The American *New Age Illustrated* series (Pendulum) brings the classics to life. This is a set of some thirty titles of classics told in pictures with limited text and captions. As condensed versions, they can usually be completed in one sitting. They can be useful in providing insight into novels that the student might otherwise struggle with. Some students follow up with the full version.

☐ The *Kennett Library* (Blackie) is a graded series in two sets, one of classics retold for schools, and the other a series of modern stories, including *The Colditz Story* by P. R. Reid and *To Sir with Love* by E. R. Braithwaite. This is a popular series, mainly with boys.

☐ The *Barcoo* series (McGraw-Hill) comprises stories set in Australia, and have plenty of action. Again, a popular set that gets the boys reading.

    ☐ Episodic books, such as *Sun on the Stubble* by Colin Thiele (Rigby, 1961), contain chapters that are a complete story in themselves. They do not require lengthy concentration or complex understanding between chapters, and the reader doesn't have to wait until the end of the book for a satisfying ending.

    For reluctant readers to put any effort into their reading, they need to experience success and enjoyment in handling books. This does not always mean having easy material to read, but finding material that matches the readers' interests and willingness to focus on the reading. Once the reluctant reader gains satisfaction from books the teacher can then find opportunities to suggest and put before the reader more demanding and worthwhile literature.

Programs with a special focus

Fairy tales and folk lore with year 7 10
Trish Ditz

In my role as teacher-librarian in a Western Australian boys' school I have ample opportunity to observe the borrowing habits of our students. Most of the older students read well and borrow extensively from our well-stocked library, but many of them rely too frequently on books of a very similar nature. I thought that if I could redirect their borrowing habits for a short time, their field of choice might become broader.

My observations of literature and language arts programs and the students' resultant reading habits had also led to my concern that our heritage of fairy tales and folk lore could be lost. Fairy tales are jolly good stories, their plots and characterisation are generally simple and direct and the action moves swiftly, with time and space unimportant. They also satisfy the human ideal of reward for fair play. I decided to direct some of the students' reading to this genre.

The year 7 students at the school are a fairly heterogenous group, some of our boarders coming from remote stations and others from overseas. Generally the students are placed in ability groups for Language Arts periods but it was decided that the fairy tale/folk lore unit would be taken with a mixed-ability group and trialled with only one of the year 7 classes.

I invited Gavin Devine, a year 7 form teacher, to assist me in the program. He was delighted, but confessed to a limited knowledge of fairy tales. His particular class had an average age of 11.7 years, with reading ability as measured on the Gapadol Reading Comprehension Test between 9.6 and 17+.

The introductory discussion

The boys were asked in our first session what they knew about fairy tales and I listed their comments on the blackboard. The following are typical:
- [ ] Stories for little children.
- [ ] Stories that start 'once upon a time'.
- [ ] Stories that end 'and they all lived happily ever after'.
- [ ] Stories that are pretty boring.
- [ ] Stories about fairies and witches.

From such comments we built up a definition of the term 'fairy tale'. The boys agreed that fairy tales have typical opening and closing phrases, the story usually involves the conflict between good and evil, and inevitably the 'goodies' are helped by some outside force because they had proven their worth.

Further questions revealed that most of the boys were unaware of how, why and where these stories came into being. All believed that they were meant for younger children and that they did not have much to offer year 7 students.

Good, I thought, this is going to be a challenge.

The students were then asked to list the titles of all the fairy tales they could remember. They were not allowed to consult any books; it was to be completely from memory. These original lists illustrated the enormous range in the children's background knowledge and experience of fairy tales: the smallest number listed was eight, the highest was thirty. The best known fairy tales, common to every list, were 'The Three Little Pigs', 'The Three Bears', 'Little Red Riding Hood', 'Cinderella', 'Jack and the Bean Stalk', and 'Hansel and Gretel'. Of these most common six titles all except 'Hansel and Gretel' are included in Roald Dahl's popular book, *Revolting Rhymes*, yet 'Snow White', which is also in Dahl's book, was only included on eleven lists. Only four students included fairy tales written by Hans Christian Andersen.

This gave me a starting point. Their lists were not very different from lists other groups of students had made using this method. I then issued a guarantee to the boys. For every new fairy tale they would read and add to our composite list, I would introduce to the class and tell or read a further new fairy tale. They all appreciated this as a form of challenge: Let's trap Mrs Ditz. I overheard, 'She'll really have to do some reading now!'.

The Little Red Riding Hoods

As a result of the original lists and their shared belief that 'all lived happily ever after' in fairy tales, I opened the second session with the following: 'You're all very familiar with "Little Red Riding Hood" — your lists have indicated that. Tell me what you know about this story'. I then recorded what they had to say on the blackboard.

Red Riding Hood
little girl
red hooded cloak made by mother/grandmother
forest
big bad wolf
woodcutters

None of the boys knew the author of this story, although a few of them were prepared to hazard a guess at the Brothers Grimm. Nobody knew the individual names of these fabulous brothers, nor how many of them there were. The boys who guessed that the Grimm Brothers wrote the story were delighted to learn that they were correct — at least in part. I had planned to read 'Little Red Riding Hood' to the class, but not the one written by Jacob and Wilhelm Grimm. (We now all knew that there were only two brothers as well as their names.) The version I had selected to read was written by a Frenchman for entertainment at the French court. I was referring of course to Charles Perrault, a man the boys had never heard of before, or so they informed me. In this uncompromising and severe version, Little Red Riding Hood is devoured by the big bad wolf. That certainly caused a stir in the classroom — they did *not* all live happily ever after.

Why then was the story written in this way? Could we relate Little Red Riding Hood by Charles Perrault to our modern day society?

After a stimulating discussion the boys decided that this was not a story for young children but was intended for young adults and that it certainly carried a lesson or warning: to be wary or mistrustful of strangers.

The Grimm version was then read. This too was a far more severe tale than the one the boys knew well. The wolf was sliced open, described in gory detail, and Red Riding Hood and her grandmother were saved by the heroic woodcutter. The wolf was later filled with stones (some of the boys recalled a similar incident in another fairy tale) which ultimately caused his death. Although Red Riding Hood was actually saved in this version, the violent and detailed treatment of the wolf caused quite a ripple and sparked off a most stimulating discussion. The boys felt that this was most unsuitable for young children. The boys' concern for the treatment of the wolf amused me, for these were young adolescents who quite openly admitted to watching violent television programs where human life was readily expended. The crux of their concern was that young children should not be submitted to this form of violence. This indicated a developing awareness and sensitivity towards the feelings of others and I was delighted with the obvious depth of concern.

One of the boys posed the questions: 'How come all the Red Riding Hood stories we know are different?' I responded to this question by discovering exactly how much the boys knew about this story. We returned to our original blackboard summary. How different were the two stories I had read to them? We set up this very basic chart.

Version	Main Characters	Action	Climax
Perrault	Red Riding Hood, Wolf, Grandmother	Visits sick grandmother, meets wolf in forest.	G'mother & RRH eaten by wolf.
Grimm	Red Riding Hood, Grandmother, Wolf, Woodcutter	Visits sick grandmother, meets wolf in forest.	G'mother & RRH eaten by wolf, but later saved — wolf slit open by woodcutter. Wolf killed by filling stomach with stones.
Well-known version	As for Grimm	As for both Perrault & Grimm	G'mother put in cupboard. Woodcutter hears RRH's calls & slays wolf.

Summary of Red Riding Hood stories

The boys all felt that the traditional Grimm and Perrault versions were quite likely considered too violent for younger children and that this must have been the reason for omitting the devouring of Red Riding Hood in later versions.

While all this concentrated activity had been directed on 'Little Red Riding Hood', the boys had been continuing their individual readings of fairy stories. We had allocated three weekly sessions of fifteen minutes duration as part of our USSR scheme to read fairy tales. As well as this the boys were encouraged to read at least two further fairy tales at home. Our lists of known fairy tales were growing rapidly at this stage with each of the boys having read at least twenty fairy stories. (Two had read in excess of seventy.)

Cinderella's themes

It was at this stage that I introduced Cinderella as our next comparative study. I read the Perrault (French) version, the Grimm (German) version and the traditional Chinese version, 'Beauty and Pock-face'.

A further chart was completed on the blackboard, and to my delight three of the boys announced that they had found a similar story in the book of English fairy tales, called 'Tattercoats'. We added their recollections to our chart.

Origin	Reason for treatment	Relationship with family	Wishes	Meets hero	Stepsisters treatment	Test
French Perrault Cinderella	Father remarries after wife's death	Stepsisters jealous, stepmother cruel	Fairy godmother	At ball one night	Forgiven – marry & live at palace	Glass Slipper
German Grimm Cinderella	Same as Perrault	Same as Perrault	Bird in tree	At castle ball – three nights	Eyes pecked out by birds	Golden slipper
Chinese Beauty & Pock-face	Mother turns into cow	Same as Perrault/ Grimm	Bones of mother in clay pot	Scholar picks up shoe on road	Roasted in oil	Walks on eggs Ladder of knives Jumps in oil
English Tattercoats	Mother dies Grandfather blames her	Hated granddaughter	Gooseherd plays flute	In forest	Grandfather's hair grows into stones	No test

Blackboarded chart comparing Cinderella stories

From this chart the boys concluded that although the versions of 'Cinderella' we had studied all differed, essentially the theme remained the same. The hard work and kindness shown by Cinderella had won through eventually, and she had found true happiness.

I was being greeted almost daily at the library by excited groups of these year 7 boys with fascinating snippets of information to pass on. They were visiting local libraries and pestering relatives and friends in their quest to find more unusual fairy tales. One of them told me that he had read that there were over 600 versions of Cinderella. Another asked me why we had not looked at any Hans Christian Andersen fairy tales yet? They were discovering Japanese, Russian, African and Arabian fairy tales — the lists were endless. They were obviously not bored.

Hans Christian Andersen's illustrators

The following lesson took up the comment relating to Hans Christian Andersen. The boys had been asked to bring along any Hans Andersen fairy tale books they could find. We discovered that he had been responsible for 156 fairy tales. 'That was better than Perrault', I was informed by a class member. An interesting comment from a boy who had shown little interest in this sort of thing a few weeks ago.

Our library had several collective volumes and some well-illustrated picture-book versions of a few of Andersen's individual stories. I wanted to use this session as a comparative study on how different illustrators interpret the same story. We had sufficient well-illustrated versions of 'The Wild Swans' to make this possible. We used *The Wild Swans* illustrated by Angela Barret (Benn), Michael Hague's *Favourite Hans Christian Andersen Fairy Tales* (Methuen), *Hans Christian Andersen Fairy Tales*, illustrated by Jiri Trnka (Orbis) and *The Wild Swans*, illustrated by Susan Jeffers (Macmillan).

The boys broke into five groups of five and concentrated on their specific book. We discovered that the language and degree of difficulty differed in each of the versions. In fact the main character's name was slightly different: Elise, Eliza, Elisa. However, the overall basic theme of the love and care the young princess had for her lost brothers was constant. Each of the illustrators had interpreted the story in his or her own style and we voted, after a lengthy and at times heated discussion, on which we preferred. Interestingly enough the boys believed that as far as literary merit went, the version contained in *Hans Christian Andersen Fairy Tales*, illustrated by Jiri Trnka, was the best. However three-quarters felt that the illustrations by Susan Jeffers depicted our ideal of the time and setting of the story most accurately.

We used this democratic form of expressing opinions quite frequently for our work on fairy tales. We developed a bar graph to indicate the boys' favorite 'baddies' in fairy tales. To achieve these final results the boys listed in order their three favorite baddies and we chose the six most frequently mentioned for our final class list. The boys again voted for three and the graph was completed accordingly from the results. Favorite baddies received three points, second on each list got two points and third got one point.

Bar graph of 'favorite baddies'

Quite obviously the boys thoroughly enjoyed the super-'baddies'. The chart caused lots of comment among library users throughout the school.

We were to use charts and graphs frequently at this stage as we discussed, debated, and then voted on favorite characters and best-loved stories. I was both surprised and delighted with the increased depth of awareness and overall knowledge of fairy tales now being shown, quite openly by the boys. The really interested group, consisting of about ten of the boys, was holding a competition to see who amongst them could read the most fairy tales. Yes, they had been right, Mrs Ditz was having to do lots of extra reading herself. However, even the weakest readers were endeavouring to find new material and they continually repeated how much they were enjoying this reading.

A theme chart

The boys had been mentioning that they could see certain similarities in many of the fairy tales they had read and heard during storytelling sessions. I directed the comments to develop a fairy tale theme chart. We all agreed that most of the stories we had become familiar with contained the following universal truths and well established values held by people: good overcomes evil, kindness is rewarded; intelligence is better than physical strength; justice is always triumphant; love always wins; hard work is well rewarded and evil people or hurtful behavior to others is dealt with in a very satisfactory manner.

I took these themes and made them into the grid included opposite. The boys were given two weeks to fill in their grids. (If you try this idea you need to limit the time to complete the checklists; you will find that whatever time you allow, your students will tell you that it was insufficient.) This in itself is rewarding as it seems to make the students more aware of what they are reading and the overall basic similarities or patterns evident in most literature.

The boys believed that themes were evident in most fairy tales and the majority felt that many modern stories were developed around such patterns. We could see evidence of these themes in such modern literature as *The Pinballs* by Betsy Byars; *Star Wars* by George Lucas and *City of Gold and Lead* by John Christopher, to mention just a few. On the basis of this discussion I prepared another grid on which we had some common titles but could add our own. Adding titles and identifying the themes made an engrossing small-group activity.

We also looked at the most frequently occurring motifs used in fairy tales. This is a fairly difficult comparative study, and so it was taken purely as a chalkboard discussion activity, using the grid below and categories that I contributed. However I believe that it can be further developed, particularly with an especially interested or talented group, so I have included a suggested checklist to foster this approach. Literary interviews (Johnson and Louis, 1985) with this age group, using fairy tale characters, are lots of fun. We also discovered fairy tale auctions could be both stimulating and expensive. The boys had to convince the rest of the class, during the auction, that their favorite fairy tale was deserving of such high esteem and value — this frequently caused riotous arguments.

A title by theme grid

THEME: TITLE	Good overcomes evil	Justice always triumphs	Unselfish love always wins	Kindness is rewarded	Intelligence is better than physical strength	Hard Work is rewarded	Unacceptable behaviour gets its just rewards
Cinderella							
Hansel and Gretel							
Snow White							
Beauty and the Beast							
Star Wars							

A grid of themes for students to complete

THEME	TITLE	HOW IN STORY
Good overcomes evil		
Justice always triumphs		
Unselfish love always wins		
Kindness is rewarded		
Intelligence is better than physical strengths		
Hard work is rewarded		
Unacceptable behaviour gets its just rewards		

Grid for motifs

MOTIF: TITLE	Magic Powers	Magic Objects	Trickery	Deceitful Beasts & Supernatural Foes	Fabulous Beasts & Supernatural Helpers	Wishes	Long Sleep Enchantment
Cinderella							
Snow White							
Wild Swans							

What was learnt?

To return to my original concern about the reading habits of the boys: they definitely had changed. We all developed markedly as literary critics during this period and the boys frequently remarked about how much they had learned. In fact some of their comments are worth quoting:

> 'I used to think fairy tales were really boring, but now I know a little bit about them, I reckon they're great.'
> 'Fantastic, fun — that's fairy tales.'
> 'We didn't meet many fairies in fairy tales — that's why I loved them.'
> 'Nearly all our stories are fairy tales.'
> 'I don't really believe fairy tales are any different from other stories, but I love listening to them.'
> 'I wish all our reading could be as fun as this has been.'
> 'Rapunzel was the first story of juvenile abuse.'

We were never bored, we really were reading individually and together, and incidentally we were living happily ever after. Well, for this year at least.

Reference

Johnson, T. and Louis, D. *Literacy through Literature*, Methuen, 1985.

Programs with a special focus

Poetry and biography   11
Sue Le Busque

In our school, the genres of poetry and biography have been much neglected as sources of reading either for enjoyment, for research about people or as a vehicle for encouraging response to literature. So as part of a library-based activity with years 6/7 children I planned a program which aimed to increase the children's knowledge, interest and response to the two genres. As a starting point, I surveyed the children to find out their preferences in reading biography and poetry. I then planned and carried out a series of activities and concluded with another survey to determine any changes in children's thinking.

The initial survey

Here are two sample returns.

POETRY

1. I ~~don't like~~ / like poetry because *Some of the poems are funny*

2. When I read poetry I feel   cross (bored) don't feel   O.K.   happy
                                              anything

3. Tick the kinds of poems you know about. Give them a rating out of 10.

   humour ✓ *5.*   animals ✓ *4.*   songs
   narrative   limericks ✓ *6½*   world
   descriptive   happenings   scarey ✓ *8½*
   people ✓ *5.*

4. What are the features of a poem that make it different from [...] writing? *Poems have verses*

5. My favourite poet is

6. If you had to do an activity after reading a poem what w[...] like to do?
   (Draw a picture)
   Find more poems like it.
   Write the poem in my own words.
   Write my own poem.

   Name *Ma[...]*

BIOGRAPHY

1. Have you ever read a biography? *yes* About whom? *Maddona*

2. I like / ~~don't like~~ to read biographies because *it is interesting knowing their hobbies and what they do*

3. If I were to write a biography I would *describe them, write their hobbies and what they do with their lives*

4. If I had to read a biography I would choose books about

   kings and queens   (actors/actresses)
   scientists   musicians   (pop stars)
   (sports stars)   soldiers   (artists)
   authors   children   doctors/nurses
   politicians   ordinary people   criminals

5. I think a biography should tell me *the most interesting parts, personalatie, hobbies and sport.*

6. If you had to do an activity after reading a biography what would you most like to do?
   (Draw a picture)
   Give a talk about it.
   (Find out more about the person)
   Rewrite it in my own words.
   (Pretend to be the person)
   (Write my own or a friend's biography)

   Name *Mary C*

From the survey I found out about the children's
- [ ] attitude towards poetry and biography;
- [ ] knowledge of poetry and biography;
- [ ] preference for particular books within these genres;
- [ ] preferred ways of responding to books.

The results looked like this:

	POETRY		BIOGRAPHY	
ATTITUDE	Positive	70%	Positive	70%
	Ambivalent	17%	Ambivalent	13%
	Negative	13%	Negative	17%
AWARENESS OF FEATURES*	Rhyme	74%	Personal information	91%
	Verse	11%	Facts	26%
			Description	52%

children could nominate more than one

I discovered that most of the children (70 per cent) had a positive attitude towards poetry for many reasons. They generally liked the subject matter, rhyme, sound of language and the feelings poems evoke. 'Poetry gives you feeling and it sounds beautiful.' Some reasons for not liking it were 'it's boring' and 'too complicated'.

A similar number (70 per cent) of children recorded a good attitude towards biography. However, when I questioned the children further it was apparent that many children had never really persevered long enough to really read a full biography. Their main reasons for wanting to read biography were that they 'were true' and 'are interesting and tell you about the person'. Once again the main reason for not liking it was that 'it was boring'.

The survey indicated that the children had a fairly limited knowledge of the features of both genres. Some children thought that rhyme was the main feature of poetry and that some poems have verses. Only a few children knew the names of poets.

For biographies, most children had strong opinions about what they would like to see in a biography, but only two showed any awareness of the author's respon-

POETRY		BIOGRAPHY	
humor	18	pop star	21
scarey	16	criminals	20
animals	12	film or sport stars	16
people	11	royalty/soldiers	9
limericks	10	artists	8
songs	9	musicians/authors	6
descriptive	8	children/politicians	5
happenings	6	scientists	4
narrative	5	doctors/nurses	2
world	2		

children could nominate more than one

*Preferences in poetry and biography**

sibility in writing a biography. These children commented that biographies should 'describe the person and his personality' and 'tell how he came to be, what he was like and what he did'. No one mentioned the need for honesty and accuracy, nor the value of biography as a source of information.

Analysis of the children's level of knowledge then gave me the information I needed to plan my teaching.

From the survey I found that many children had preferences for particular kinds of poems and for biography subjects.

The popular choices in poetry were scarey and humorous ones. For biography, pop stars led the field, with criminals a close second and acting and sporting stars third. I thought these results were fairly predictable, except for the criminals.

The results of the survey showed that most children liked to illustrate or draw a picture as a response to both genres. Only three children said they liked to do written responses to books.

POETRY		BIOGRAPHY	
draw	19	draw	19
further reading	0	give talk	3
rewrite	1	research	13
write own	0	rewrite	1

Preferred means of response

There was a lack of variety in what children might want to do in response to a book and this led me to try to think up some interesting alternative responses in order to boost appreciation and understanding. I did not feel that drawing a picture encouraged either very much reaction or interaction with the material and noted that no children chose further reading as a response to a book.

Planning the program

Using the information from the survey, I planned specific teaching goals, the material to be used and different responses to try out. I decided to begin with poetry of the kind already well liked by the children, and to introduce ideas about poetry and some alternative means of response around these poems.

The poetry sessions

The first six sessions were on poetry. My aims were to increase the children's knowledge of poetry, to introduce different forms of poetry, various features of poetry and to learn about some well-known poets. I also wanted to enrich children's understanding by encouraging different kinds of responses to poetry. We spent three sessions studying the ways in which lines, verses, rhyme and rhythm can be used as we listened to limericks, scarey poems and funny poems.

Scarey poems
Michael Dugan   Bamboo Tiger
Jack Prelutsky   The Ghoul
Jack Prelutsky   The Vampire
We tried a dramatic activity in response to 'Bamboo Tiger'.
Humorous poems
June Factor   *Far Out, Brussel Sprout!* (a selection)

Clare Scott-Mitchell *Apples From Hurricane Street*
Edward Lear   *The Pobble Who Has No Toes*

As a response activity we did further reading.

Limericks We read selections from

Myra Livingston   *A Lollypop of Limericks*
William Cole   *Oh, What Nonsense*
William Cole   *The Book of Giggles*

We wrote limericks as a response.

Two sessions on narrative poems were next. We discussed the features of narrative poems and talked about some well-known by the children.

Narrative poems

'Banjo' Paterson   *Mulga Bill's Bicycle*
'Banjo' Paterson   *The Man From Ironbark*
Robert Browning   *The Pied Piper of Hamelin*
Alfred Noyes   *The Highway Man*

We tried rewriting *The Pied Piper of Hamelin* as a story and dramatised *The Highway Man*.

In the final poetry session, we looked at some well-known poets and their work. The children responded by researching a poet in groups and reading more of their work. We read poems by Roald Dahl, Doug Macleod, and more old favorites.

1 Scarey poems
    Teaching points: feature — rhyme, lines, verses, rhythm.
    Response: Make a play of the poems (in groups).
2 Funny poems
    Teaching points: rhyme, lines, verses, rhythm.
    Response: Further reading.
3 Limericks
    Teaching points: distinctive features of limericks (patterns).
    Response: Write some limericks.
4 Narrative poems
    Teaching points: long, tell a story, verses.
    Response: Re-write the poem as a story.
5 Narrative poems
    Teaching points: many verses, tell a story.
    Response: make a play of the poem.
6 Poets
    Teaching points: works by well-known poets.
    Response: Research and further reading.
7 Biography
    Teaching points: features — should include childhood life, anecdotes, birth and death details, family, why famous, interests, hobbies, personality.
    Response: Oral discussion of story read aloud.
8 Biography
    Teaching points: Author's responsibility — accuracy, honesty, research, create interest, describe.
    Response: Silent reading.
9 Biography
    Teaching points: as above, revision.
    Response: Silent reading.
10 Biography
    Response: Silent reading and critical review.
11 Biography
    Response: choose from a list of responses given — research person read about; draw; pretend to be person read about; interview person (write questions you would ask); write a biography; re-write the biography you read.

Planning the program

Reading poetry

The biography sessions

We began the biography sessions by discussing the features which should be included in a biography, such as an account of childhood life, details of birth and death if appropriate, description, anecdotes and discussion of why the person is famous. I read a life of Lady Jane Grey to the class and we talked about whether it contained enough of the features of a good biography to make it interesting reading. The children agreed that it did. In the next session we talked about the author's responsibility to be accurate, honest, and thorough in research and presentation when writing biography. The children then began reading biographies from a selection provided.

I had some difficulty in supplying sufficient biographical books about the people selected by the children. Many of the pop stars who are currently popular have not been around long enough to have had books written about them. I located very few books on criminals which were written at the children's level. Two biography series which I found useful were Hamish Hamilton's 'Profiles' and Ashley Mallett's series on sports stars. My biography reading list looked like this:

Jeremy Pascall	*The Cinema Greats*
Ken Piesse	*Donald Bradman*
Johanna Reiss	*The Upstairs Room*
Francene Sabin	*Louis Pasteur: Young Scientist*
Kevin Shyne	*The Man Who Dropped from the Sky*
Kim Stevens	*The Bee Gees*
Dick Tatham	*Elton John*
R. J. Unstead	*Men and Women in History*
F. M. White	*Escape! The Life of Harry Houdini*

During the next two sessions the children read and discussed the biographies they had chosen. I asked them to take note of whether the author of their choice was including features of biography and keeping to the responsibilities of a biographer. At the end of the fourth session, by which time the children had finished reading, short critical reviews of the books were written. In the last session the children were presented with a list of possible follow-up options.

Response to literature

Activities for promoting response to literature included both oral and written. Many of my ideas for response came from *Word Magic* (McVitty, 1985) and *Literature Ideas for Upper Primary* (Queensland Department of Education, 1984).

POETRY	BIOGRAPHY
Drama Further reading Original writing Rewriting as a story Research	Research Draw Role play Role play (interview) Write an original biography Rewrite a biography

Activities children could select

I wanted the response activities to extend the children's understanding and enjoyment of the books they read. I hoped that dramatic activities such as making up a play or role-playing and rewriting activities would indicate how much children understood of the author's intent. The writing activities were designed to allow the children to experiment with the particular features of the genres, and the opportunity for further reading and research allowed me to see whether children were involved and interested in reading more in the two genres.

When studying the children's responses to the literature sessions two aspects were considered:

☐ which kinds of response produced the most engagement with books; and

☐ which kinds of response were most enjoyed by the children.

In most cases children responded to literature in groups. They worked in groups to plan and present the dramatic activities, and worked in pairs or threes for the role plays. In the writing activities children conferenced each other and shared ideas. Research was also shared when children had common interests, while further reading was done individually.

Observing the level of interaction during the various responses, listening to the children's comments and/or planning activities, watching or reading the end product of the activities and just talking to the children were all good guides to how the children felt about the piece they had read. However, more careful in-depth analysis of the reaction or level of enjoyment of the response can be tricky at times. Studying facial expressions, the degree of involvement and the quality of work produced can be a good informal guide, however I found that some children are quite adept at 'producing the goods' in order to satisfy the teacher. I found that some of my observations about enjoyment were not supported by the results of the later survey. For instance, although children appeared quite involved in the written responses for poetry and produced some interesting work, very few listed written response as an activity they preferred.

I found that drama led to considerable involvement. In planning how to act out poems the children had to interpret the author's intentions about plots, setting, feelings, sequences and themes. The children particularly enjoyed this kind of response. There was a high degree of involvement and the plays were of a high standard. Oral discussions were also enjoyed by the children. These discussions are a good way of producing interaction and are a useful way for the teacher to gauge children's responses. It was difficult to observe interaction or reaction during further reading, as the only way to determine involvement was by studying children's faces while they read and to look at how much reading they did. Illustrating appeared to require very little interaction or involvement and I still wonder why this remained as a preferred response.

Written responses were useful in gauging the children's level of interaction with a book and also helped children learn various literary features. For example, writing their own limericks led children to a much better understanding of the craft of using lines, rhymes and rhythms. Rewriting a poem as a story required understanding of different genres in the same way as planning a play. Writing critical reviews of biographies needed lots of interaction and involvement but many children did not seem to enjoy this activity even though the reviews were of a high standard.

Planning and performing a play

The follow-up survey

The survey I gave out at the end of the sessions was designed to find out how the children reacted to the various response activities and whether their knowledge of genres had changed. I used the same questions on poetry as for the first survey but modified the biography questions. I found there was little overall change in attitudes to poetry; however, the children's awareness of poetry as a genre had increased considerably. I do feel that the level of involvement required for the various response activities contributed greatly to this. There were now many more children aware of the features of poetry and of particular poets' styles.

A sample from the follow-up survey

BIOGRAPHY

1. I like / ~~don't like~~ to read biographies because *they are interesting to read and you get to know more about the person.*

2. If I were to write a biography I would *right a biography on Madonna Louise Ciccone.*

3. I think a biography should tell me *all about that certain person from childhood to adult hood.*

4. Which activity did you do? *write about Madonna*
   Did you enjoy it? *yes I did*
   Would you do a different one next time? *Yes I suppose*
   If so, which? *Brian Manix*

Name *Mary C*

| | Percentage mentioning | | | | |
	rhyme	rhythm	verse	lines	poets
Before	74	0	11	0	40
After	57	27	35	42	50

Children's knowledge about poetry

It is interesting that fewer children mentioned rhyme as a feature. I suspect that I made a point of stressing that not all poems have rhymes.

Changes in attitude to biography were more significant. Five children who had said they would like to read biography changed their minds. The general feeling amongst the children was that 'the books are too long to read and are sometimes boring'. I feel that one of the problems with biography was the lack of availability of suitable books. During oral discussion, I found that most children preferred the kind of potted biography found in magazines. On the plus side, four children who voted against biography in the first survey now said they liked it.

At the beginning of the sessions only a few children had a clear concept of biography and now all knew what biography was all about. One wrote that the author of a biography should 'write about the fantastic life and about the person's personality (but) some pictures are boring'. Another said authors should 'write interesting facts in a story form'. Many children felt that some authors do not fulfil their responsibilities as biographers. One child commented, 'I think they are very boring. I would rather read Judy Blume's books'. Another wrote, 'if the person's dead it would not make a happy ending'.

Interestingly, children's preferences for response had moved away from illustration.

Preferred response	Poetry Percentage mentioning		Biography Percentage mentioning	
	Before	After	Before	After
drawing	88%	69%	74%	50%
further reading	0%	20%	52%	30%
write in own words	4%	11%	4%	0%
drama	0%	46%	44%	20%

*children could nominate several responses

Preferred responses to literature

The children nominated fewer choices in the follow-up survey for responding to biographies and I think the lower score for written work was because they did not enjoy writing the reviews.

Conclusion

I think the program was successful in increasing children's awareness of the genres and ways of responding to them. The greater choice of response activities did not have any effect on the children's attitude to the genres but the different ways of responding certainly enriched the experiences of children who disliked the traditional forms of drawing or writing. For myself, I found that drama and oral discussion produced the most interaction with material, while drawing a picture produced the least.

The program only ran for a short time but I think it showed that variety in response can lead to more interesting and enjoyable literature sessions and that some response activities provide greater learning opportunities than most others.

References

Decker, M. *100 novel ways with book reports* Scholastic, n.d.

Hooper, W. H. *Guidelines for middle school use of the library*, Brisbane Education Centre, 1981.

Hooper, W. H. *Guidelines for upper school use of the library*, Brisbane Education Centre, 1982

Hathorn, Libby *Good to read, 5*, Methuen, 1982.

Hathorn, Libby *Good to read, 6*, Methuen, 1983.

Hill, Susan *Books Alive! Using Literature in the classroom*, Nelson, 1986.

Literature ideas for upper primary, Queensland Department of Education, 1984.

McVitty, Walter (ed)., *Word Magic. Poetry as a shared adventure*, Primary English Teachers' Association of NSW.

Thomas, Ron *Into Books. 101 Literature activities for the classroom*, Oxford, 1984.

Walshe, R. D. (ed.) *Teaching literature*, Primary English Teachers' Association of NSW, 1983

Programs with a special focus

In the library with Roald Dahl   12

Beverley Endersbee

As a teacher-librarian I worked with a year 5/6 class for several weeks using a literature-based program with Roald Dahl's books. Although the children were engaged in a rich language program in their own classroom, most of the work we did with Roald Dahl's books was done in the library. Several children had already read and enjoyed some of Dahl's books so I planned to introduce as much of his work as possible and have the children respond to Dahl's stories through a wide range of activities: poetry, art and craft, photography and keeping a writing journal.

I knew that I wanted to achieve the following:

- ☐ introduce children to the author, Roald Dahl;
- ☐ encourage children to respond and interact with literature in a variety of ways;
- ☐ model positive reading behavior to show that I personally enjoyed reading;
- ☐ develop children's positive attitudes to reading longer stories;
- ☐ monitor and evaluate the children's attitudes to reading.

Getting under way

At our first session I explained to the children that they were to continue having their library session with me on Monday, but that I was also going to read to them every morning from 9.05 to 9.25, except on Thursdays when most of them went to choir. I was going to read aloud a number of Roald Dahl's books in this daily time slot, and on Monday afternoons we would do some fun things based on Dahl and his books.

This first information session took place on Monday morning. During the afternoon session I gave the children a writing journal in which I glued a sheet about how the journal was to be used.

THIS BOOK IS A PLACE FOR YOU AND ME TO TALK ABOUT BOOKS, READING, AUTHORS AND WRITING. YOU'RE TO WRITE LETTERS TO ME AND I'LL WRITE BACK TO YOU. IN YOUR LETTERS TO ME, TALK WITH ME ABOUT WHAT YOU'VE READ. TELL ME WHAT YOU THOUGHT AND FELT AND WHY. TELL ME WHAT YOU LIKED AND DIDN'T LIKE AND WHY. TELL ME WHAT THESE BOOKS MEANT TO YOU AND SAID TO YOU. ASK ME QUESTIONS FOR HELP. WRITE BACK TO ME ABOUT MY IDEAS, FEELINGS AND QUESTIONS.

A sheet explaining how the journal could be used

The sheet is based on an idea by Nancie Atwell (*Language Arts* 61, 3, 1984).

During the session we discussed the children's ideas of what keeping a writing journal might entail, and agreed on several things:

- ☐ the children could write to me about anything, not just books;
- ☐ the children could write about other books and characters, not just the stories I was reading;
- ☐ the children could write to me;
- ☐ I would write back to them;
- ☐ as soon as they arrived on a Monday they would just grab their journals and write.

They were quite excited with the thought of *me* writing back to them! For this first Monday I got them to write to me about their thoughts about reading, and anything else they wanted to tell me.

Sharing response journals

Watching the children begin to write provided some useful information about their attitudes to reading and to writing. Three children had great difficulty in getting started. They were most reluctant to put pen to paper. I told them not to worry about the spelling of words, just to have a go and let me know what they thought. This helped them get started but what they wrote was minimal. Another three 'special' children, who are bussed in to attend our special education class, were completely 'hung up', perhaps through lack of confidence, so I scribed their thoughts. Most children however had no trouble at all and relished the idea of writing to me, and several children wrote more than one page. Two of them wrote all over their book covers (shades of Penny Pollard!).

I was keen to see what the children had written, and I responded to them all that night. Sure enough, next morning four of the children wanted to read their journals, so I was glad I had responded quickly; I believe it showed them that I appreciated what they had written and I was able to quickly gain their confidence. I always responded on the Monday night just in case they wanted an early reply.

Introducing Roald Dahl

In the next session I began reading aloud *The BFG*, a surefire winner, and a book the children responded to positively; I heard groans when I got up to leave, and there was total absorption with eyes glued on me and ears taking in every word.

When we had progressed far enough into the book we had some ideas about activities we could base on the story. We decided we particularly liked Roald Dahl's way of making the giant, the BFG, talk. In fact this way of speaking was already creeping into several of the children's vocabulary. We started by exploring the BFG's use of 'spoonerisms' and 'poor' grammar. We decided to turn nursery rhymes into spoonerisms, and write them out on giant feet shapes.

The BFG lent itself to many, many other activities, not all of which we could use. One of these was the suggestion that we have a whizzpopper competition in the library during lunchtime!

We soon settled down to a set pattern for Monday afternoons. I would blackboard some ideas and the children could choose from various activities. I felt this set pattern maintained a form of continuity, even though a week had passed between these activity sessions. The daily readings were vital though, to keep up our contact as a class and to hear more of Dahl's writing.

The blackboard activities looked like this at the start.

1 Read my response.
2 Respond back to me.
3 Do a rough copy of your spoonerism.
4 Show me your completed copy.
5 Do your good copy, add your name, display.

As we got further into *The BFG* there were more options for the children to choose from BUT there were two rules — you must do your response, then finish last week's choice of activity before beginning a new choice. I kept a list of names and the activity they chose, so I could record and check on the work speed of the slower children. It wasn't long before there were several activities going on at once.

Some of the early activities the children and I came up with were:
- ☐ do an acrostic poem on a giant foot;
- ☐ design a crossword;
- ☐ design an alphabet/counting book using words/ideas from *The BFG*;
- ☐ use the thesaurus/Guinness Book of Records for giant words/giant 'things';
- ☐ draw part of a giant (for example, part of an eye, a nostril or a big toe) for a rogue's gallery.

Some children developed a film script on the BFG, others made BFG alphabet books and others developed a puppet play.

Some beginning activities

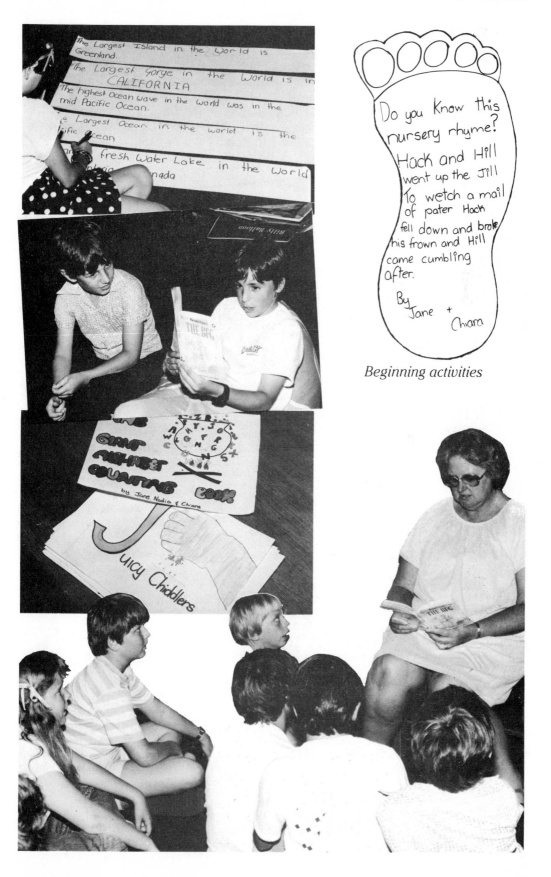

The Largest Island in the World is Greenland

The Largest Gorge in the World is in CALIFORNIA

The highest Ocean wave in the World was in the mid Pacific Ocean.

The Largest Ocean in the world is the ...ific Ocean

...ar... fresh Water Lake in the World ...nada

Do you know this nursery rhyme?

Hack and Hill
went up the Jill
To wetch a mail
of pater Hack
fell down and broke
his frown and Hill
came cumbling
after.

By Jane +
Chiara

Beginning activities

More Dahl books

Once I had finished reading *The BFG*, I read two of Dahl's shorter books, *Revolting Rhymes* and *The Enormous Crocodile*. Again it was obvious that tremendous spinoffs in all curriculum areas could have occurred daily if I'd been the classroom teacher.

Next I read *George's Marvellous Medicine*, *The Twits*, *The Witches*, and finished off with Chris Powling's magnificent review, 'Roald Dahl', which answered many of the questions we'd just posted off in a letter to Roald Dahl himself.

Norwood Primary School
96 Beulah Road,
Norwood. 5067.

Dear Dahl's Chicken,

We are a group of abnormal Year 5/6 chiddlers from Norwood Primary School which is in Adelaide (The Grand Prix City) in South Australia, where we taste like Anzac biscuits (from the story "Possum Magic" by Mem Fox). We've been listening to several of your stories and felt we'd like to know more about you. Firstly we would like to know where you get your ideas from e.g. why are they funny, why are the people ugly, do you see people walking down the street and they give you ideas for a book. Once you've got he ideas how, when and where do you start writing? Is your writing a job or a hobby? Do you write at a certain time? What age did you start writing? Did you like writing stories in school? What is your favourite story out of those you've written? Our favourite is "Revolting Rhymes" followed by "The Witches". What was your favourite book and author as a child? Some of ours are yours, Enid Blyton, Robin Klein, J.R.R. Tolkeen, Gene Kemp, E.B. White. Did any other authors influence your writing? We don't think you have because nobody writes as well as you do!

We love your style of writing, especially in the B.F.G., especially the spoonerisms and poor grammar that the B.F.G. uses. Do you think like that or was it hard to get the idea? Left or right?

We love Quentin Blake's illustrations. Did you choose him or did your publishing firm? We think he is just great! Does he live near you? Do you tell him what part of the story to illustrate or does he read the story through and decide what needs illustrating? Have you been to Australia? If not, why not? Have you any ideas buzzing around in your head for a new story?

Have a Happy Xmas and a safe New Year.

From your friends,

and typists, Shannon and Anthony

We've just bought and are reading Chris Powling's story about you but we still wanted to write to you. (The teacher - Bev Endersbee)

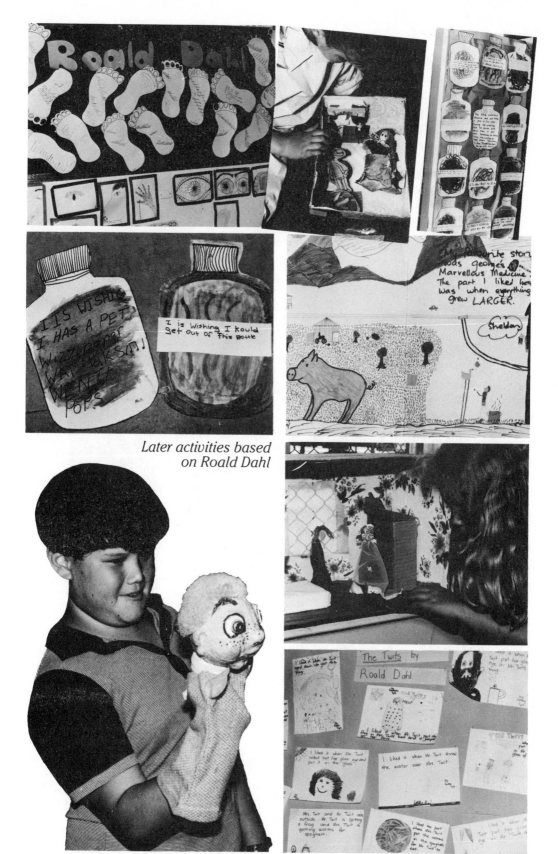

*Later activities based
on Roald Dahl*

More activities

As time went by the children's options for activities in response to all Dahl's books became more varied.

☐ Design a cover for a book or your journal, of the favorite part of your favorite story. Write why you chose this particular part of the story and add these comments to your drawing.

☐ Write a filmscript story board and film your script if you wish and turn it into a book.

☐ Make a diorama of a part you have enjoyed.

☐ Write giant book reviews on large pieces of paper for other classes to read.

☐ Make up one question for a quiz, *Sale of the Century* (based on the TV show).

A Sale of the Century quiz

The children's response

The journal-writing was enjoyed by all the children, and they always responded enthusiastically on a wide variety of topics.

I also saw evidence of how the children enjoyed the journal writing in the way more than half of them would arrive, regularly, anything up to fifteen minutes early for our Monday lessons. Either they were eager to do their response or get on with their activities, which couldn't be done until their responses were written down. I wonder which?

One of the boys, Adam, would write back to me using an invented style of writing and spelling, obviously BFG-influenced! He changed my name to EndersBFG and responded to me using that name!

The journals were used for a wide variety of dialogue between the children and myself. They did not always contain reference to books, although I usually tried to include at least one or two questions related to the story I was reading to them and/or they were reading to themselves, for example, 'what did this book/character make you think of?'. On reflection, I probably did not ask enough open-ended questions. At times I also asked the children to evaluate the stories I was reading to them by having them make comparisons with previous stories and suggested they give the stories a rating out of ten.

```
                                    well        now      I'm
   readin    the    Bo BB esey      twins
 wonerfulll      secquet        wierdo  storie
 for    dat    I  was,      wieadin
 wilburs   smiths .   The    Sunbird
   ex      storie
     in    the      holis     I     was
   went     to    Vicitori  harborie
   I  wented  to     de      bluff
   I    waz
 sikillderfull   reel    happy     dere
   there    for    place      we      stayed
   I    went      to    daisies
 fried    eggs    to  ther  show   on
 salad    day    day    an
   thowbage           I   got  4
   rest    ob   did    nutin   the
       the  days         bye
                      from   Adam
                      (me)
```

```
   Is   this   B.F.G.   talking ?    Is  fried
 Eggs  Day  (Friday)  and  Salad  Day  (Saturday)
 if  so  that's  very  clever !!
       Yes  the  Bobbsey  Twins  is
 different  to  your  last  book.
 Wilbur Smith's      I'm  surprised  you're  reading
             books.
```

Some reflections about the programs

Journal responses

I feel it was a pity the journal responses were weekly, as the time-span between children writing and reading my reply was too long. I believe that the format I tried would be better suited to a classroom program as more time for writing, more continuity with classroom activities and more daily observations of the children and their interests would have made the journals really good. However, as it was, there was close communication achieved on both sides.

Time

The time problem was also evident in the activities section of our Monday sessions. In fact, the dioramas caused such a fantastically positive response, with the children unwilling to wait week after week to complete them, that their class teacher kindly let me have the children for two other class times to finish them. The dioramas have caused great interest amongst the whole school. They are on display in the library and the other children are busily discussing which is their favorite.

Literature activities

Whilst enthusiasm was very evident for most of the activities, I'm sure that by the time each Monday came around some enthusiasm had waned, not with the small quicker activities, but with some of the larger ones that tended to 'drag' on. However, no one really complained or said they didn't want to complete their choice.

What did the children think?

I used informal observation and also more formal methods to assess children's attitudes to reading. I observed and listened to children at play, at lunchtime and when conversing with their friends. I also used the more formal attitude scale, the Heatherington Primary Scale as described in Alexander and Filler's book *Attitudes and Reading* (International Reading Association, 1976). To complete the attitude scale a child reads a question prefaced with 'How do you feel . . .'. The child chooses one of five answer responses and those answers are given a numerical value between one and five. There are twenty questions and the answer responses are marked on the face that best represents how the child feels.

The attitude scale shows the teacher which children have positive attitudes to reading and which have a more negative attitude. It also enables you to find out what kind of reading the children like and where they like to read.

The questions asking children to record their views on 'reading at the library' received the highest positive rating in 15 out of the 21 papers.

Summary

I had several aims when I started on this project.

One aim was to introduce the children to Roald Dahl's books, and to Roald Dahl as an author. I think this aspect was very successful, as was the aim of modelling 'good' reading habits. We have twenty copies of Dahl's books in the library and none of them are in, so that's a positive sign. I hope they all come back!

Another aim was to foster positive attitudes to reading longer stories and whilst most are reading longer stories, I should have done a survey first term to be able to say that they have really achieved this aim. Still, I think it has reinforced for the children the notion that reading books is fun.

A further aim was to do a variety of literature-based activities about Dahl's stories, and this we certainly did; *but* I still feel that even greater benefits would have accrued to the children if the program had been classroom-based or done in a team teaching 'block' approach with more interaction with the teacher. Close liaison with the classroom teacher is essential for any library-based or literature-based program. Next time I hope this will be possible.

About the authors

Trish Ditz is a teacher-librarian at Guildford Grammar Preparatory School in Western Australia. She has taught in Victoria as a primary school classroom teacher and also as a History and English teacher at the secondary level. Trish believes that it is important for language learning that literature be the catalyst for the total language program.

Bev Endersbee is a teacher-librarian at an inner suburban primary school in Adelaide. She has been a classroom teacher for fifteen years and a teacher-librarian for the past eleven. Bev believes that books provide a multitude of starting points for integrating reading, talking, art and drama.

Kathleen Graham has been a teacher-librarian with the South Australian Education Department for seven years. As teacher-librarian in Adelaide's northern satellite city of Elizabeth, Kathleen has had a special interest in fostering children's literacy. This interest has led her to help set up literature-based reading programs in the last two schools in which she has worked.

Meredith Kennedy is in her sixth year as a part-time teacher-librarian. Like many teachers she is looking for ways of bringing books and children together so that the children find in books inspiration for their own creativity.

Helen Kerin has been teaching middle primary children for eleven years in city and country schools. Recent post-graduate studies changed her approach to teaching reading. She is now convinced of the benefits of a literature-based approach. Helen is currently a peripatetic teacher at the Elizabeth Special Education Unit, north of Adelaide.

Sue Le Busque has taught in Victoria and New South Wales and is now the teacher-librarian at Newtown Primary School in South Australia. Sue came to believe that reading is 'caught not taught' after watching her own children learn to read.

Joelie Hancock is a lecturer in Language Arts at the South Australian College of Advanced Education, Sturt. She is a strong proponent of reading programs that focus on the readers' enjoyment and response. Joelie is currently developing a data base of children's literature to be used in classrooms. She is Editor of the *Australian Journal of Reading*.

Susan Hill worked as a junior primary teacher for many years before taking up an appointment at the South Australian College of Advanced Education, Magill. Two key interests of Sue's have long been how to enthuse children about books and how to extend what they gain from reading. She completed a doctoral thesis on developing reader response and recently published *Books Alive* (1986), a book on ways to extend children's responses to what they read.

Shayne O'Halloran has taught in New South Wales and Canada and now works in the Northern Territory, where she has a year 6 class at Malak School in Darwin. Shayne has had extensive experience in teaching children from homes where they see little reading and writing. She believes that classroom teachers play a vital role in developing children's reading attitude and preferences.

Andrew Phillips has been deputy principal at Lock Area School in the Riverland of South Australia for the past fifteen years, where he has been actively involved in both the primary and secondary programs. His external studies in school librarianship and reading education have both furthered his interests in literature. Andrew has seen the success of a variety of basal reading schemes in teaching children how to read but he is firmly convinced that a literature-based approach best fosters an interest in reading that students carry beyond their years at school.

Pat Smith is a senior teacher at Beaufort in Victoria. She has worked for an untold number of years as a teacher, including three years as a teacher-librarian and another three years as a language consultant. She believes that there is great value in basing an integrated oral language, reading and writing program on literature.

Deirdre Travers is a teacher-librarian at Mercedes College, Adelaide, where she works with teachers and students from Reception to year 7. Deirdre believes in the value of discussing books to extend students' emotional response and also to help them form connections with the classroom curriculum.

Maria Woodhouse recently completed a graduate diploma in reading and language education. Maria believes that developing confidence, self-esteem and enthusiasm for books is paramount in a reading program. She has found that a literature-based reading program is successful in changing the attitudes of children who were turned off books. Maria recently shifted to Perth, where she is currently on leave and enjoying her baby daughter — to whom she reads every day!

Shirley Yeates trained as a primary teacher in Victoria, has taught in a variety of schools as a classroom and remedial teacher in the south-east of South Australia where she is now part Language Arts co-ordinator and part classroom teacher at Seaton North Primary School. Her post-graduate studies in reading and language education supported her conviction that a literature-based reading program is the most successful and enjoyable way to teach reading.